Ye Olde Torrington Days
A Collection Of Writings
by Paul Bentley

ISBN-13: 978-1539729785
ISBN- 10: 1539729788

About The Author

Paul Bentley is a freelance writer and the author of the sort-of memoir *Sh*t A Teacher Thinks (and sometimes says)*, the novels *All Blood Runs Red* and *August Descending,* and three other compilations of essays and feature pieces: *My Torrington Days: A Collection Of Writings, More Torrington Days (Volumes 1&2), and Torrington Days Forever*. All are available on Amazon. He lives in the Northeast with his wife and the great cat Ivy.

To all my friends and acquaintances, past and present. You have never left me.

Table Of Contents

The History Of THS Baseball
The Earliest Years: 1895-1909

(*The Torrington Voice*. August 10, 1995. After researching the history of THS basketball and football, it was only natural that I would add baseball at some point. Eventually I wrote about the earliest years, and included in the original article, in column form, 100 years of won-lost records from 1895-1995, coaches, captains, and tournament results. Those stat columns are not included here. This turned out to be the lone article in my THS Baseball "History.")

Baseball is for every boy a good, wholesome sport. It brings him out of the close confinement of the schoolroom. It takes the stoop from his shoulders and puts hard, honest muscle all over his frame. It rests his eyes, strengthens his lungs, and teaches him self-reliance and courage. Every mother ought to rejoice when her boy says he is on the school or college team.

– Walter Camp, 1889

The On Deck Circle
Played midst the background strains of chirping crickets and of whinnying horses on dirt thoroughfares. Amidst the clackety-clack of trolley wheels traversing Main and of church bells pealing up-and-down Wolcottville and across the Green. With factory whistles screeching the noon hour and parlor pianos belting out "Take Me Out To The Ballgame" and "After The Ball Is Over," baseball in late 19th century Torrington brought townspeople together in an outpouring of athletic pride.

It was back before the telephone connected residents of our fair borough. Back before automobiles allowed for easy visiting or the radio gave us almost instant news of our neighbors. Back even before there was a local newspaper to link its derby sporting, corset wearing, parasol toting citizens to the latest news and gossip and thus instill a sense of oneness, of community.

Torringtonians gathered then, as they do now, in shaded evenings after work or on sun blistering weekends to watch and participate in baseball. To cheer uniformed family and friends. To root, root, root

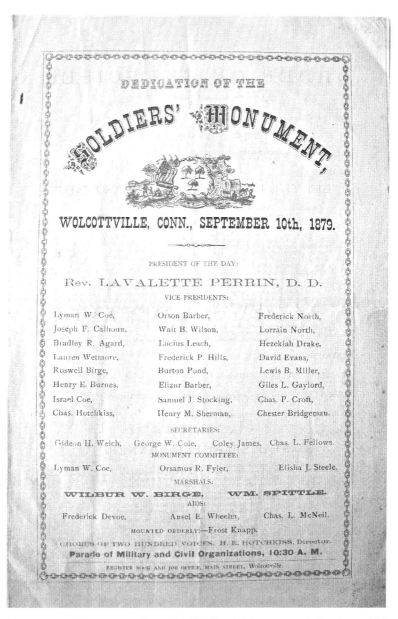

DEDICATION OF THE

SOLDIERS' MONUMENT,

WOLCOTTVILLE, CONN., SEPTEMBER 10th, 1879.

PRESIDENT OF THE DAY:

Rev. LAVALETTE PERRIN, D. D.

VICE PRESIDENTS:

Lyman W. Coe,	Orson Barber,	Frederick North,
Joseph F. Calhoun,	Wait B. Wilson,	Lorrain North,
Bradley R. Agard,	Lucius Leach,	Hezekiah Drake,
Lauren Wetmore,	Frederick P. Hills,	David Evans,
Roswell Birge,	Burton Pond,	Lewis B. Miller,
Henry E. Burnes,	Elizur Barber,	Giles L. Gaylord,
Israel Coe,	Samuel J. Stocking,	Chas. P. Croft,
Chas. Hotchkiss,	Henry M. Sherman,	Chester Bridgeman.

SECRETARIES:

Gideon H. Welch, George W. Cole, Coley James, Chas. L. Fellows.

MONUMENT COMMITTEE:

Lyman W. Coe, Orsamus R. Fyler, Elisha J. Steele.

MARSHALS:

WILBUR W. BIRGE, WM. SPITTLE.

AIDS:

Frederick Devoe, Ansel E. Wheeler, Chas. L. McNeil.

MOUNTED ORDERLY:—Frost Knapp.

CHORUS OF TWO HUNDRED VOICES. H. E. HOTCHKISS, Director.

Parade of Military and Civil Organizations, 10:30 A. M.

REGISTER BOOK AND JOB OFFICE, MAIN STREET, Wolcottville.

(Above, an 1879 program from the Soldiers' Monument dedication. This "monument" *is* the Civil War statue which now stands at the north end of Coe Park. The dedication occurred in the same general time period that baseball was beginning in Torrington.)

for the home team. They gathered, and the sense of Torrington as a "team" soared out beyond white-limed foul lines and advertising-splattered wooden outfield fences. Soared to the very outreaches of the town itself.

Baseball was the earliest of all "ball" sports to be practiced here in the valley. When exactly it began is impossible to say. There was no Wolcottville newspaper till 1874, and then a fire in 1881 destroyed the earliest copies. What is left from 125 years ago is very little.

(An early motorist on upper Water Street circa 1900 no doubt on his way to a ball game. Note the shadows of the onlookers and photographer in the lower right.)

Baseball was certainly being played in Torrington by 1870. There is in the Torrington Historical Society a receipt for baseball shoes purchased by W.E. Brady for the Aetna Base Ball Club. There is also a small 3½ x 5½ yellowed scorebook from 1874 mentioning Torrington and area teams like the Nutmeg BBC (Base Ball Club), Empire BBC, and Meteor BBC. Torrington names such as Coe, Hotchkiss, Wheeler, Dayton, Dwyer, O.R. Fyler (scorer), Kennedy, Dillon, Brothwell, Brooks, Ryan, and F.R. Matthews (umpire, also ran the Torrington Opera House for years) began being linked to the games. . . In 1888 something known as the Fat Man Team of Torrington played, humorously pairing its name with the sedentary nature of the sport itself. Whether any of the men (Dennis Murphy,

William Friend, Frederick Alldis, et al.) were actually "fat" seems irrelevant. They were baseballers and part of the lineup that helped carry Torrington baseball teams into the 1890s and into schoolboy history. Game time for THS.

Play Ball!
The first THS class (below) graduated in 1889, and by the gay

(The THS Class Of 1889. L-R: Emma Andrus, Margaret Sherman, salutatorian Lucy Miner, Sophronia Coe, valedictorian George Alvord, Ellen Joy, Gertrude Hall. Graduation was on June 26; the principal was Edwin H. Forbes. Note: Most likely there were students who completed high school level course work before this, but this was the first "official" graduating class.)

1890s the students were ready to take to the diamond. Unfortunately it is impossible to say with certitude exactly what year they started.

It is reasonable to deduce that the first THS team trotted onto the field in 1891. In that year there were at least 2 teams of businessmen (John Brooks, John Calhoun, Dr. Pratt, et al.) in Torrington, and the newspaper made mention that there was talk of challenging the "School" nine. They probably did, and probably lost. The businessmen could not have been too good. Reports of their playing mentioned that many of them injured their fingers which, while not uncommon in this era, does not get mentioned aside from the businessmen. . . In 1894 the THS Tabula waxed nostalgically about that 1891, saying, "The base-ball reports which are now filling the columns of our exchanges bring to mind pleasant memories of our own victorious nine which made its successful career in '91. It was a nine well worthy of commendation of any High School. Many were its victories and few its defeats."

Part of the problem with getting information this far back lies in the fact that THS was small and was not yet a power player in local news. Much THS news, no doubt, went unheralded by the school and team itself. And thus went unreported, i.e. promote not, get not. . . Another problem would be the sort of "unofficial" nature of high school sports in the 1890s. Though THS might have fielded a team in 1891, it is unlikely they had uniforms, paid officials, or played any games outside town sandlots. For one thing the school was too small to justify much, if any, athletic expense. Example: In 1891 THS graduated a mere 8 students, only 2 of whom were male. Moreover, the asking price to rent the Athletic Grounds (later Fuessenich) was too high for even some of the older and better teams. . . A third part of the problem regarding sports information rests with *The Evening Register* itself. Back in the 19th century our local newspaper was a thin, 4-page daily that once-a-week was expanded into a larger news-of-the-week version. It is only this expanded edition that has survived on microfilm, i.e. it's entirely possible that high school sporting events got reported in the thinner daily press, but were edited out of the weekly summaries, though I could find no mention of THS sports in the one box of dailies which still exist.

The bottom line on the origins of THS baseball is that most likely there was an unofficial, unsanctioned baseball team in 1891. And that *that* team played a game that was remarkably similar to today's. The bats were, of course, wooden and less tapered. Balls were deader, and gloves looked like swollen caricatures of human hands. But it was *still* a contest of 9 innings, 3 outs to a side, 3 strikes to an out.

After 1891, according to the little I could find, THS next fielded a team in 1895. The ninety-fivers beat the Business Men that spring 13-9 (without mention of injured fingers). THS baseball reappeared again in 1897. That '97 team beat Campville 7-2 and the Nameless Nine (Litchfield) 12-6. In the Nameless Nine victory, THS turned its first ever recorded double play, though the student reporter groused, "The decisions of the umpire were very yellow and caused lots of kicking. He gave Nameless Nine much assistance." THS lost the season's closer 16-11 to the League Of American Wheelman. Wall's absence was cited as a reason for the loss, thus establishing the first official documented excuse in THS's long baseball history.

In 1898 two games were played against Gilbert, but no results were given. This was the first recorded contest of interscholastic play. I naturally assume Torrington won.

There was no team in 1899, but there was an interesting newspaper article about some boys playing baseball in the Migeon lot north of the Needle Shop on Field Street (must be where the parking lot is today). Apparently they were annoying residents by chasing foul balls over lawns and trampling flowers. A Mrs. Weston made a mad dash for the ball the final time it was hit into her yard. As she stooped down to retrieve it, one of the boys tried to kick it away but instead kicked her in the mouth "making the blood flow freely." The boys got away just before the appearance of Mr. Weston. The news report didn't mention who got the ball.

On February 17, 1900, a meeting was held to form a baseball club, and it was said to be the "first ever at THS." Though THS had played baseball on-and-off since 1891, this date marks its official beginning. Uniform colors were debated, and a rule was passed that only members would be allowed to participate, perhaps implying that in the past non-matriculated athletes had filled in.

The season began with 3 consecutive victories before losing 6-5 to the older players from Waterbury HS. The season closed with a victory over the local T.A.B. Note: The Total Abstinence and Benevolence Society was comprised of males who were older, bigger, and more experienced than the high school lads. The T.A.B. would be a frequent THS opponent in baseball and basketball throughout the early years. And they usually won. The reason they didn't in 1900 could be summed up in 2 words: Tad Quinn. And he would be back for 1 more season.

The 1901 season was arguably the best season THS ever had. The team finished 9-1, was referred to as the "Invincibles," had a "stonewall infield," and clobbered such schools as New Britain HS (16-3), Waterbury HS (12-0), and even beat an older and greatly experienced Coe Brass team (2-1). Many fans stayed away from the Coe Brass game expecting it to be "a farce." But Quinn allowed only 5 scattered hits, and later when the THSers went around to merchants soliciting money, they received $80. A winning high school nine was considered a credit to the town and good for business. It was just smart retailing to support the baseballers. The only loss in 1901 came at the bats of Gilbert (score, 6-3), even though Quinn struck out 16. THS immediately issued a challenge for the rubber match (THS had beaten Gilbert earlier). When Gilbert declined, THS officials then issued a challenge to take on any team in the state to decide a state champion. When all declined, THS claimed a state title. The final balance of $18 in the treasury was spent on an outing at Highland Lake. A team picture (below) was taken and submitted for publica-

(The 1901 THS team. Front Row, L-R: H. Ellis, Harry Friend with a young black who might be the bat boy. Middle Row: Ben Mulligan, Tad Quinn in dark sweater and gripping the baseball in a tossing pose, Chamberlin, Art Lawton. Back Row: Holley, C. Fuessenich, Jonas. NOTE 1: Unfortunately this photo came to me with the right side cropped out. Missing are players Halloran and Blake Fuessenich, *and* Manager Bernhold. NOTE 2: The money which was raised is conspicuous in the new equipment to include uniforms, quilted pants, spikes, flat style hats, a catcher's mask, chest protector, bats, gloves, etc.)

tion in the 1902 Spalding Guide. It had been a great season!

Clarence "Tad" Quinn was an amazing THS athlete. He was big (6'1" and over 200 pounds), had a fine curve ball, and was once described as "the Matthewson of the high school aggregations."

Against New Britain in 1901 he struck out 22 and also led the THS in batting (.375). In 1902 he was called up to Norwich, went to the Majors that same year, and stayed with the Philadelphia Athletics for 2 years. In those 2 years in the Majors, he pitched in 3 games, 17 innings, struck out 4, and gave up 23 hits with an ERA of 4.76. Sidebar: Quinn was 2 for 6 at bat in those games for a .333 average. Perhaps his true forte at that level was as a batter. In any case he soon came back to Torrington and continued to be a positive influence around THS. He coached the football team for 3 years and ultimately died in Waterbury at age 64 in 1946.

THS baseball games of this era were played at the Athletic Grounds, later known as League Park, later still Fuessenich. It was important that the park be a money-making proposition, as it was feared the owners would sell it off as building lots should it not be. The rental rate for organizations in 1906 was $17.50 for 20 games. Admission was 15¢, the grandstand 10¢, and ladies were admitted free of charge. To avoid paying, many spectators used nearby gardens and woodsheds as vantage points. Damage was done, complaints lodged. The Athletic Grounds and right-of-ways were eventually fenced in.

For a period the high schoolers had no formal field to work out at, as the Coe Brass team (Below, the 1910 Coe Brass state champs)

(Front Row, L-R: C. Brimble, Kenney, Doyle, Iver, Thompson, Hoar. Middle Row: McLeod, Tommers, Duke, A. Brimble, Conroy, Baldwin. Back Row: Gilmartin, Sager, Maynard, Homer.)

practiced at the Athletic Grounds each afternoon. With no other *regulation* fields in existence, the THS team had to resort to evening practices. In 1914 the regular diamond was in such rough condition from overuse and maintenance neglect that a temporary diamond had to be roughed out in the outfield. The uneven ground seriously affected fielding, and THS pitcher, Captain W. Harold Dowd, in 1916 gave up 12 runs in the first inning.

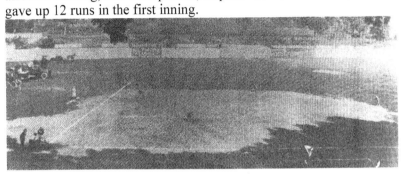

(Above, early baseball action circa 1910s at League Park/Fuessenich. Note the parked automobiles and the advertising on the outfield fence.)

Early teams traveled by trolley, train, and horse-drawn livery rigs. Because of the extravagant time that travel took, the "ball tossers" liked to take a little extra time off from school. When the issue came to a head in 1903, superintendent Forbes ruled that there would no longer be baseball on school days without special dispensation from the board of education. Then, to cut the "bag runners" some slack, the superintendent ruled that THS would be in session on Fridays only from 8 a.m. to 1 p.m. And that the boys could play after that.

Studies always came first; only students proficient in their classes could play. In 1904, two players were ineligible for the opener, but played anyway. In addition that year Captain Albert Wheeler and Manager Holley picked up 2 "ringers," i.e. hardballers who weren't even students. The board quickly stepped in and took drastic action. It had to. This was the same sort of questionable tactics that THS had accused other schools of. The board forbid the THS team to play under the school name. Thus in 1904 the season was officially over, though the opening "victory" over Waterbury HS was never officially forfeited. Sidebar: The THSers *did* reorganize under a different name and *did* manage to play 2 more games (losing both) before losing interest in a season that could not be played for the dear old Church Street school.

Good times were never far afoot from a THS baseball team. The 1902 team led by Captain Charles Brimble followed up the 4-3 season by giving a performance at City Hall consisting of scenes from *Merchant Of Venice*, along with vocal and instrumental music. It was said that there was much talent along the Baseball Association members. The 1906 team, under the direction of Manager Mayhew Baldwin, went to Bristol by rail and took along a train car of rooters and THS girls. THS lost to Bristol HS that day 21-20 and committed 15 errors. *But* one can assume they had a lot of fun on the train ride. . . In 1908, the same year that the 40-ton boulder was moved from West Torrington to Coe Park, the 3-1 baseballers painted a cliff at Highland Lake despite having no rope. They used grapevines. Again the next year the enterprising horsehiders (final record 4-8) reprised the feat and painted a large "T" at Junction Park at Highland Lake during an end-of-the-year picnic. There apparently was something about unpainted granite that drew the neophyte Torrington baseball spirit to it.

Question: As those ball players swung out over the cliff's edge suspended in space and only held by a fiber-dry brown vine, did they hope to suspend time too? Did they hope that a large white luminary "T" would cause future generations to look up when they passed and think of young THS boys once again alive beyond the sun-dappled sky into which they stared? Alive and still laughing, still tossing hardballs around in Elysian fields forever green, forever ringing with the sounds of THS baseball?

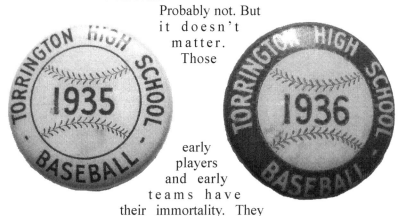

Probably not. But it doesn't matter. Those early players and early teams have their immortality. They were the pioneer spirits that began it all. Began the winning legacy of Torrington High School baseball.

(A THS warmup jacket from the 1990s.)

8

A Few Of My Favorite Things

(*The Torrington Voice*. August 22, 1996. Though 20 years have passed since I wrote this article, I am as enamored as ever with Torrington and the opportunities she offers to be active and entertained. Some of these businesses are no longer with us, but the idea is the same, i.e. if you're bored in Torrington you have no one but yourself to blame. Sorry.)

Real Scene #1: "I only came back because my mother was sick, and I had to take care of her," the native Torringtonian told me. "Now that she's gone, there's nothing to keep me here."

"Goodbye," I said disinterestingly. . . **Point:** If you don't like it here, there are roads to all points of the compass heading out, some even without potholes.

Real Scene #2: "I didn't want to come back from Florida," the new YMCA worker told me, "but my wife wanted to spend some time with her parents. Me, I hate this town."

"We didn't miss you when you were gone," I pointed out dispassionately. "And we won't miss you if you leave again". . . **Point:** Unless you have super glue on your soles, there's nothing binding around here, not even referendums.

I hate it when people bad mouth Torrington. The type who constantly project the WC Field's attitude: "I went to Philadelphia (Torrington), but it was closed."

There are *lots* of things to do right here in T-town, *or* very close by.

I love the geography of hills, valleys, lakes, streams, i.e. we've got a backyard Sierra Club. Nothing to do? Go tubing on the Farmington, canoeing on the Housatonic, fishing in the Naugatuck. Take a rock climbing course at NCCC. Try swimming at the Besse Pond pool, hiking around Burr Pond, running laps at the THS track or cycling the West End hills. In the winter there are ice fishing and skating, sledding, downhill skiing, snowmobiling, snowshoeing, lap walking in the Armory, cross country skiing – all guaranteed to stimulate blood flow and work up an appetite.

Hungry? Thirsty? Have a Sam Adams at The Pedlar, some sausage Florentine at Dick's, a plate of antipasta at The Venetian, a pizza from Anthony's, a calzone from Roma's, and a cannoli or cream horn from Lombardi's. As long as you're downtown pick up a Torrington afghan from Donna Weigold at The Country Shoppe and see what Jeff Drucker at Coins and Collectibles wants for a limited edition Wetmore brick. Finally, swing by City Hall and ask the mayor to nullify your parking ticket should the retailing excitement make you forget the time.

It's true Torrington lacks jai-alai, team equestrian, dog racing, hydroplane racing, curling, world class opera, and world cup bungee cord jumping. But you can take in a great collegiate baseball game at Fuessenich (and even wear a cool Twisters hat like the one below), a movie, a ballet, or a play/ national act at the Warner. . . If spectating isn't your thing, try joining a bowling or pool league, competing in a 9-5 tournament, signing up for a choral group or Adult Ed classes. There are a teen center on Albert Street, a senior center across the street, service clubs, fraternal organizations, sororities, dance and acting troupes, etc. etc. Even a sporting Fish & Game group on Weed Road that hasn't shot any members, or anyone else, yet. . .

Still nothing catching your attention? Try George Burns' formula: "Happiness? A good meal, a good cigar, and a good woman – or a bad woman. It depends on how much happiness you can handle."

If you're still shaking your head at all this, you're not jaded or bored. You're dead. And for that we have LaPorta, Phalen, Gleeson, Hillside, New St. Francis, Center, St. Peter's. . .

(Former *Torrington Register* reporter, sports editor, editor, and publisher for 50 years, 89-year-old Walter "Walt" Gisselbrecht relaxing at home in Torrington in 1997.)

Walter "Walt" Gisselbrecht
Newspaperman Extraordinaire

(*The Torrington Voice*. April 24, 1997. It's no secret that there are extraordinary individuals living among us in Torrington. Many of them senior citizens who, for lack of self promotion and a world caught up in the *now*, spend their remaining days forgotten and many times alone. I've written on a number of these citizens over the decades. I wish I'd written on more. Walt Gisselbrecht epitomizes the sort of individual who, though forgotten by most, had a huge impact on Torrington and its people.)

He could be described as the great pater of valley journalism, specifically the journalism of Torrington. He began writing for *The Torrington Register* the day after he graduated from high school. And he didn't stop for 50 years. He wrote in an era of manual typewriters, of wire services coming over automatic telegraph machines on Morse code circuits, and of Simplex presses. *The Register* was an afternoon paper, and in his earliest years, results of such mega-events as The World Series would be hollered out via megaphone to throngs gathered in the Water Street parking lot.

Walter "Walt" Gisselbrecht lives quietly today with his daughter and son-in-law, Ann and Bob Amicone on Visconti Avenue. His hobbies are the sedate, intellectual ones that one would expect from a life lived nose deep in newsprint.

"I like books," Walt Gisselbrecht recently told me. "I always did. I still read a lot. I still read *The Register*, *The Courant*, and *The Republican* everyday." The printed proof was within arm's length of his favorite chair. When asked what his guiding philosophy was from his newspaper years, he replied unhesitantly, "I just tried to do my best."

Just trying to do his best began inauspiciously for young Walt. He was born on February 23, 1908, on Calhoun Street, 1 of 10 children to August and Josephine Gisselbrecht. His father was a carpenter and cabinetmaker, his mother a housewife. The heritage was German, but Walt's earliest memories were all-Torrington.

"I remember when the Armistice was signed (1918). I was 10. Everyone congregated in the center. There was nothing formal, just haphazard stuff. The trolleys were still running." As the years rolled on, Walter became deeper-and-deeper inculcated with things Torrington. Early teenage was spent with Troop 2 Boy Scouts at Trinity Church with patrol leader Seymour Weeks. Education too was local: North School, Wetmore, THS. "Principal Jeffries was strict, but fair," Walt said remembering the long ago THS head. "Teachers were strict too; they had the authority. We went to school morning and afternoon, and we had about an hour and 15 minutes for lunch. There was no cafeteria. I walked home to Calhoun Street. Kids from out-of-town brown bagged it. Students didn't have cars; we walked everywhere. We had sports, and once in awhile there was a dance in the old high school. There was also Agard's for dancing, and the main place for refreshments was the Olympia just north of Agard's on Main."

It was the Roaring Twenties. Life was robust, a heady moxie elixir for the teenage Walt Gisselbrecht. At THS he was the manager of the track team, and he played football (middle right side of photo). "I was a substitute on the first undefeated team THS ever had. I played for 2 years (Note: 1924 & '25 were both undefeated, though there were 5 ties). Tracey Garey was the coach. He was a good athlete who tried to do his best. Local businessman Jack Williams helped him. In my senior year we spent a week at Camp Mohawk training. Fay Vincent and Ducky Pond helped out."

Walt Gisselbrecht substituted in enough games to earn a letter and a gold football senior year. Though not a stellar athlete, Walt participated, gave it his best, and *that* is the salient point. He was not by nature passive, but rather charged with kinetic energy. A young man who wanted to be in the forefront of any passing parade. Accordingly, in a 1925 Tabula he was portrayed as being "one of the most popular boys in our class. He is studious, ambitious, and a good fellow." The same article talked of his "terpsichorean activities in the junior cloakroom." It was said that "he made his noted rival Rudolph Valentino look sick," that "would-be sheiks quailed at the sight of Walt," and that "cake-eaters wept in despair at the mention of his name."

It was a humorous, tongue-in-cheek portrayal of a young man already being marked as an up-and-comer. And Walt reciprocated in the same, good natured vein when he wrote The Class History Of 1925. He spoke of Ethel Croft and Alice Peasley experimentally weaving each other's hair. Of "Jumbo" Gertrude Aust leaving a permanent dent in the floor after a fall. Of talkative Richie Chaplin being assigned an essay: "The Manipulation Of The Lower Jaw." Walt's history is humorous, but it is also perceptive and inclusive of all the prerequisites for a newspaper future. The 17-year-old showed a memory for events and quotes, a penchant to be cuttingly funny but not harsh, an ability to turn an original phrase, and mastery of basic and more advanced English.

The latter was a fact not lost on him even 72 years later. "I've been told that graduating from high school in the early twenties was worth a bachelor's degree today." Whether or not such is the case (and I do *not* believe it is), THS was the last formal education Walter would receive. Those years served to hone his writing skills, and as time would show, the training was pivotal.

❖ ❖ ❖ ❖

"The day after I graduated (June 1925), I went to work at *The Register*. A couple of weeks before, the editor, George Peterson who also lived on Calhoun Street, had his son tell me that his father wanted to talk to me. I went over; he was eating breakfast at the time. He told me to see him the day after I graduated. He said years later I was the only guy he ever hired eating breakfast. . . I think he had been talking to Jeffries, and I think Jeffries gave me a good recommendation. I started at $15 a week."

In 1925 few went to college. Most in Torrington went into the factories.

But Walt Gisselbrecht went to 190 Water Street. George Peterson

(Above, an original wooden sign)

had seen the newsman within the boy, and Walt himself was astute enough to follow his natural propensities. Columnist Mike Pearl noted in a 1993 issue of *National Review*, "Newspapers used to be staffed with men who rode the subways and trusted their own judgment." Seventeen-year-old Walt Gisselbrecht walked in and trusted Walt Gisselbrecht. He was a natural fourth estate man.

In 1925, The Torrington Register's editorial staff consisted of: George Peterson, editor; John Thompson, city-editor; and Harry Knickerbocker, Matt Beary, and Arthur Bonalumi, reporters. Walt Gisselbrecht became the 6th man. "At that time you did everything. Someone had to write sports; I was elected. It didn't make a differ-

ence to me what I wrote. Later on, around the early 1940s, I stayed mostly in the general news end."

In 1925 Walt Gisselbrecht began covering the Torrington sports beat. Soon, in addition to beat coverage, he was also turning out a daily column on everything from national and state athletics, to the clarity of the Y water. For example, "The YMCA swimming pool is in excellent shape this fall. The water is as clear as glass – so clear that the tiles on the bottom can be counted by a person with ordinary eyesight."

Walt was everywhere: THS sports, the factory leagues, the A.C. contests, etc. And what was a *Register* reporter's life like? "*The Register* was an afternoon paper until 1968. We'd start around 8 a.m. and go to press around 3-4 p.m. The newsboys would get the papers right after. The staff would come in evenings if there was a story or happening to work on. John Thompson was a nice guy. It was more-or-less like family. Everyone was cordial. We socialized a little outside the office. They were *all* Torrington people."

In 1931 Walt Gisselbrecht married his high school classmate, though not sweetheart, Evelyn Brenker. The couple moved into a Blake Street rent and at some point in the thirties bought a car ("We didn't travel much before then."). Eventually they moved to Lyman Drive where they had 2 children: Anne and Walter. It was here that the couple spent most of their 53 years of married life till Evelyn's death in 1985.

(Above, photo circa 1947 at the family cottage on Tyler Lake. Walt is on the far right, wife Evelyn behind him, son Walter in front of him, and daughter Ann the tall girl in front.)

Career Highlight: "One of the things I enjoyed most was during WWII, Jack Maylott the executive director of the YMCA, Jiggs Donahue of *The Waterbury Republican*, and myself organized "News From Home" which we sent to all service people. It was a 4-page newspaper: general news, sports, and a column about the service people themselves. We wound up sending out over 4000 a month to area servicemen. The Community Chest sponsored us. Once a month groups of women and girls would come down to the Y to address envelopes. We had the support of the community too. Once we got a letter from a GI on the front lines in Europe. He'd found our newspaper on the ground and wanted to be put on the mailing list."

George Peterson died in 1947/'48, and John Thompson was made

(The Register staffers gather in the newsroom in 1927. L-R: managing editor John Thompson, editor and publisher George Peterson, composing room helper Dante Mazzochi, AP telegrapher Raymond H. White, business manager James W. Peterson, reporters Walter Gisselbrecht and Harry W. Knickerbocker, and wire editor Matthew W. Beary.)

editor. He lasted only a couple of years before he too, the prolific "Thom," died and was replaced by Walter Gisselbrecht. Walt in addition to being named editor, also became business manager and held the dual positions until 1968 when the Register was sold to the Millers' *Berkshire Eagle*. From 1968 to his retirement in 1975, Walt Gisselbrecht was publisher, the culmination of a 50-year, uninterrupted newspaper career.

And what kind of boss was Walt Gisselbrecht? Long time journalist Owen Canfield: "Walt hired me. I had just graduated from Palmer Institute Of Authorship (correspondence course, GI bill) in 1960. I remember that first interview so well. I'd answered an ad for a reporter. Walt hired a college degreed applicant first. I was so discouraged. Three months later he called me back and asked, 'Would you like to give it a try?' Would I! Walt gave me my break. He was always an advocate for me. He let me write. He was the first nuts-and-bolts, good English proponent I had. He would brook no screwups. He wanted good, straight English."

And was Walt Gisselbrecht tough? I asked Owen. I'd detected some flint when I'd taken Walt's arm on the stairs at one point in the interview, and he told me he could manage himself. Canfield: "When push-came-to-shove, Walt could be tough. He'd let you argue, but when time was running out, toughness." But, Canfield implied, toughness tempered with old fashioned, gentlemanly consideration. Canfield: "In my first year, THS was built. I was an eager beaver and went down to Wetmore and talked with John Hogan (superintendent). We talked for a long time how the new high school would be the George Vogel HS, or so I thought. Walt met me the next morning at 6:45 a.m. 'You made a mistake here boy,' he said kindly. It was embarrassing for the paper. Walt himself ran the retraction that day in a front page box, but didn't mention my name."

Politician Delia Donne, whose first job was as a teletype operator at 190 Water Street, said, "Walt was very kind, very soft spoken. He was a gentleman and was very considerate of his employees."

From 1925-'75 Walt Gisselbrecht dealt with people, and he dealt with the stories of those townspeople. I asked him if any of those stories, those archives of copy he tapped out manually on some staccatoed Remington for half a century, stood out in his mind. With the self-effacing modesty of a man who's met more deadlines than a modern syndication, he said "no" but added, "The flood of 1955 was a big story. We had no power and didn't publish for 7 days. I was information officer for the Civil Defense, so when the flood came, I worked at City Hall as public information officer. I did miscellaneous jobs for (mayor) Bill Carroll, wrote press releases, and worked with the Salvation Army. There was a lot going on."

A lot going on. For Walt Gesselbrecht there was a lot going on from the time he stepped into *The Register's* newsroom in 1925 till that day in 1975 when the Millers gave him a parting handshake and a brass-plated mantle clock run by atmospheric pressure. It still spins silently on his hearth today. Over the years he's been secretary of the Connecticut Sportswriters Alliance, and treasurer and later president of the Connecticut Daily Newspaper Association. He's VP of the Historical Society, serves in a variety of Torrington agencies in a variety of capacities/high posts, and is a member of several fraternal organizations.

We spoke for a couple of hours. Walt Gisselbrecht was fighting a slight cough, but his steadiness of thought and diplomatic cordiality was old world. He told me some stories that by 1997 standards were quite innocuous, but insisted they be off-the-record.

Before we parted, he said, "I enjoyed working with people." His simple declaration was apt and key to the man. From 1925-'75, then as now, *The Torrington Register* was not without its detractors. I've heard criticism that it was too insular in its news coverage, that it was too provincial in its unwillingness to tackle sensitive issues, that it was too inbred answering to sundry, familial-tied interests.

But, in the end such indictments soften when one realizes just what the old *Torrington Register* under Walt Gisselbrecht did. It covered people. There's not a microfilmed or bound yellowed copy that is not teeming with people in the headlines, photos, news stories, press releases, etc. If you cover people, you cover a town. People *are* the town. And if you cover those people humanely and fairly, as gentlemen and inherently good newspeople do, then you ultimately pass on worth and dignity to the town itself.

Torrington became a better place for Walt Gisselbrecht's 50 professional years. I'm not sure that Walt himself ever reached the potential he showed as a 17-year-old writer. I think he could have been big. But his energies went into building a newspaper, a town, and its townsfolk instead of concentrating on deification, an apotheosis of self.

Seventy-two years ago THS senior Walt Gisselbrecht wrote: "I want to suggest that we take for our life motto: Whatever you do, do well." Quod facis bene fac.

He did just that.

Rest In Peace - Walter Gisselbrecht
(1908 - 2001)

(Young man Walt with cut-
off shirt sleeves and work gloves
helping out at a family clambake.)

(Walt at Trinity Church in 1946 holding
his niece. Evelyn is to his right.)

(Walt at home in 1997.)

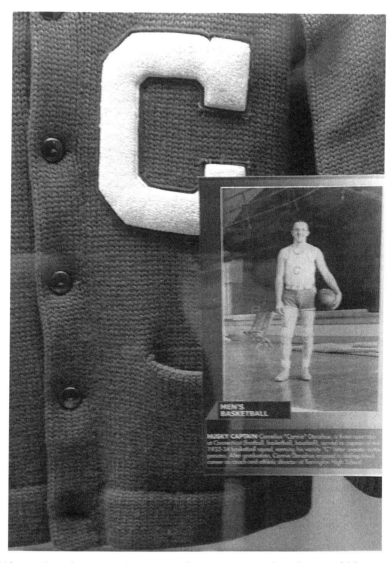

(Above, Donahue's varsity Connecticut sweater and a picture of him as a basketball player. They're displayed behind glass in the J. Robert Donnelly Husky Heritage Sports Museum on the Storrs campus. The caption beneath his picture reads: "Husky captain Cornelius "Connie" Donahue, a three sport star at Connecticut (football, basketball, baseball), served as captain of the 1933-'34 basketball squad earning his varsity "C" letter sweater in the process. After graduation Connie Donahue enjoyed a distinguished career as coach and athletic director at Torrington High School.")

Cornelius "Connie" Donahue
Sportsman Par Excellence

(*The Torrington Voice*. May 1, 1997. Was there a more well known name in Torrington from the mid-1920s through the early 1970s than Cornelius Donahue, a.k.a. Coach Donahue, a.k.a. Connie? I doubt it. When I decided to write a few articles on senior citizens, it was a no-brainer to include the affable Irishman. Like Peter Dranginis, Tom F. Wall Sr., and Walt Gisselbrecht, all of whom I also wrote about, Connie Donahue was everywhere, knew everyone, and had prodigious recall. It was an easy interview. A special thanks to Connie's son Tom, who furnished a number of these photographs.)

A Frank Merriwell shot by Connie Donahue from the side of the court with but 2 seconds remaining to play gave the THS basketball team a 25-24 decision over the Drury High courtsters of N. Adams, Mass. at the state armory Saturday evening.
– The Torrington Register, Dec. 5, 1927 –

Sports and the excitement associated with it: last second shots, goal line stands, grand slam homeruns, have all been the essence, the fiber, the spiritual marrow of the man Torrington has known as "Connie" and "Coach" for three-quarters-of-a-century. He was weaned on a Grove Street sandlot; passed pubescence fighting for St.

Francis; gamed-on through his teen THS years. He became a young man on the hardscrabble, Depression Era playing fields at Storrs. And entered adulthood back at THS where he coached for 37 years. The active show closed in 1972 (Right, Connie in a '72 classroom) with retirement. But the leading man never left the gymnasium. He recast himself as audience member and attended the collegiate Final Four for the next 20 years, went to high school and UConn games, enjoyed media sports via the expansive Laurel Cable, and talked sports incessantly to

anyone with a similar bent. In his earlier years, young Cornelius was told by his mother, "All you ever talk about is sports." The descriptive became prescriptive, and the bruised-kneed boy became *the* sportsman.

Cornelius "Connie" Donahue was born on October 17, 1909, at home at 23 Grove Street, Torrington. The family consisted of 3 boys (Connie, Harvey, Bill) and 1 sister (Evelyn). Connie's father worked at Turner & Seymour foundry, a tough environ at the south end of the old trolley line. He died when Connie was 5. "My mother (Anna) kept us all together. We went to live on North Street where Gus Hanson and other Torrington athletes lived."

(Above, the Donahue family in 1961 at a celebration of Connie's 25th year in coaching. Front Row, L-R: wife Rose, Connie, mother Anna. Back Row: sons Tom and Dennis; siblings Bill, Evelyn Gleason, and Harvey.)

It was an era of tight-knit neighborhoods with a sandlot on every corner. "There was a Doyle's lot on Riverside. The Torrington Company lot where Connie Peasley and Red Germano played. Mumy's lot with the Peerless AC, Freddie Woodlin, George Ganem, and a cripple batboy named Jimmy Angus. And, of course, there was Fuessenich. The Spear Street gang and the Hogan brothers controlled that." Connie and his neighbors played ball in the vacant lot on Grove, and the action was of the indigent, Spanky and Our Gang type. "We played in rags. In football we used black socks stuffed with rags for padding. In baseball the bat was held together by nails and tape, and the balls were always taped. I didn't own a baseball glove until high school."

The Grove Street lot itself furnished as much excitement as the on-field sports action. "The river near Grove would flood," Connie remembered, "and we'd have to get the chickens out of the stream. Balls would go into the river. A fellow got swept downstream once, and some guy jumped off the E. Pearl bridge to save him. We'd dam the river and go swimming. Warrenton Woolen Mill would release dye every so often, and we'd have to post a lookout who'd yell, 'Dye's coming!' so we could get out of the river."

Young Connie in those years saw John Murphy (future superintendent), Fay Vincent, and Bus Pond play. He lived in the shadow of Torrington greats like Jim Hogan, Yale man Tommy Burnell, Tom McLeod, and 1915 THS captain Barb Daly who was reputed to have hit a homerun to straightaway center at Fuessenich, 555 feet. Connie knew the men, knew the stories, and it was all Crackerjack manna to his young sports soul. He himself played under increasing scrutiny as he got older, the unbridled sandlot energy and raw talent falling occasionally under part-time, pseudo coaching in the upper elementary years. At that time there was an Elementary School League, and in 1925 St. Francis with a young Donahue defeated a Pivots Pavlicovic led Sacred Heart for the basketball title.

Entering THS in the autumn of 1925, Connie wasted no time trying out for football. There was no freshmen or JV team, so it was

CORNELIUS DONAHUE
"Connie"

Baseball 1, 2, 3 4
Football 2 3, 4
Basketball 1, 2, 3, 4
Captain of Baseball 3
Captain of Football 4
"His athletic powers speak louder than words."

(Above, Connie's 1929 yearbook photo.)

varsity or nothing. "I made the varsity thanks to Ducky Pond. We had a scrimmage one day, and Pond took note of me. He told Coach Garey, 'That kid ought to be on the team.' " By junior year Donahue

27

was playing tackle at 160 pounds. "I told Coach that I shouldn't be playing tackle at 160. He told me there was no one else." Laughs. "Of all the sports, I liked football best. I loved to play defense." The love showed. Senior year Donahue was voted captain, made All-NVL, and received honorable mention for All-State.

Connie Donahue also played 4 years of varsity baseball and basketball. In baseball he held down 1st base and was selected as captain junior year. In basketball, freshman Connie became known as

Eighth Annual 1926
National
INTERSCHOLASTIC
BASKETBALL
TOURNAMENT

MCH.
30-31
APRIL
1-2-3   UNIVERSITY
of CHICAGO

another Bill Ski (Szeskowski) and went with the second Wonder Five to the National Tournament in Chicago in 1926 (team picture on p.65, left is a souvenir program). "We were given $15 spending money and a necktie. In Chicago, Dutch Clark (later a pro quarterback) was the first player I ever saw shooting one-handed. The shot came from up high. After we got beat, we went to Washington and saw a baseball game between Princeton and Miami, and later stopped off in NYC. It was quite a thrill."

The kid from Grove Street was going through life with eyes wide open and was getting an education that far outreached the Church Street school. Part of that education came in the form of summer employment. Times were hard for the fatherless Donahue clan, and though mother Anna worked and other family members helped out, teenage Connie was expected to do his part. "One summer I worked on the railroad for 40¢ an hour. Mr. Shugrue, who was head of Section #42, said to my mother, 'I'm going to give your boy a job.' I was going to be the waterboy, but I learned how to spike, raise the rails, and use tamping bars to keep the tracks level. Shugrue told my mother, 'He's good, but he eats half my lunch.' Every Friday we'd get in line to be paid. I was last. They'd all sign Xs for their names."

In 1927-'28 when Torrington Country Club was being built, Connie and 25 boys from THS went up there to work. "We pulled out bushes by the roots. After 3 days, there were 4 of us left. I was determined to stay. We were poor, and I was determined to help out mother. Bill Ormsby and Pops, we built the tees and greens. Another summer Mrs. Pequignot got me a job for Serkey the plumber digging ditches. Another summer I peddled ice."

It was real life weight training and a real life odyssey of will. Many adult men didn't measure up. Cornelius seemed to be thriving. Legendary sportswriter Grantland Rice, back in this same 1920s gloaming, wrote, "For when the One Great Scorer comes to mark against your name, he writes, not that you won or lost, but how you played the game." Connie Donahue was playing the game of life with the same indomitable spirit that won him acclaim on the athletic fields.

Following THS graduation, Connie traveled north to St. Bonaventure for a football tryout. The players were older, bigger ex-miners, and they played football with the same relish usually reserved for hitting rock with sledge hammers. Connie came home, took a year off (essentially red shirting himself), and went to work for Procter & Gamble in Waterbury. He became a door-to-door salesman demonstrating free samples. His boss Jim Welsh became a surrogate father to him. Connie with a trace of regret said, "I never really knew my own father." Connie memorized a routine/pitch, some of which he still knows. And whenever possible took rival Palmolive's samples and left his own. He developed a palate for German cooking at downtown Drescher's Restaurant.

In 1929-'30 Donahue matriculated to the Ithaca School of Physical Education and played on the freshmen basketball team.

(The ISPE freshmen basketball team. Donahue 3rd from left.)

The following fall in 1930, Connie Donahue transferred and entered UConn as a forestry major and immediately reported for football. "I started for UConn that first season, but I tore ligaments. Freshman year I also broke my leg sliding in baseball. The bone was sticking up, but the trainer set it perfectly. The called me 'Crutches.' I was on those crutches off-and-on for 2 years. Sophomore year I got voted Best Defensive Lineman. I got kicked in the kidney, peed blood, and had to go to the ER in Willimantic. The kidney was ruptured and had to come out. I was critical for a while. As it turned out, my body never had used the ruptured kidney, and my other kidney was twice normal size. It was the reason I was never able to gain weight above 160 pounds (at 5'11"). After the operation, I started to sprout and went up to 210."

Connie played guard in football for 2 years, guard in basketball (3 years and captain), and outfield in baseball (3 years). "I wasn't fast. Baseball was my best sport. Sumner Doyle was my baseball and football coach. He lived to 103." FALLACY: Connie Donahue was the first 3-letter varsity athlete in UConn history. FACT: There were other 3-letter athletes before Donahue, like Pop Williams. But there weren't many.

After 3 semesters Connie changed his major to education and PE, and in June 1934 he graduated. There were no jobs, so he worked on

campus that summer, and in early fall 1934 got a government job in forestry in Kentucky. "It was one of Roosevelt's programs. My mother wasn't too thrilled. 'You're not going to go down to that wild country, are you?' she asked." The 25-year-old adventurer bought a Model A Ford, hit the road, and met his fellow lumbermen in Sterling, Kentucky. And mom was right; it *was* wild. "I saw Lil Abners while I was down there, but no Daisy Maes," Donahue said smiling. "There was a rattlesnake on the cabin wall; I hate snakes. There were no improved roads, just dirt roads that ran ridge lines. We surveyed the land and estimated the amount of timber. I ran into a lot of hillbillies and squatters.

Generally the hillbillies were nice people and always liked to talk to you. They raised hunting dogs and kids, and they were farmers and moonshiners. One time we went off the road and heard bullets going overhead."

It was Connie's Master Degree in roughing it and survival, i.e. in life.

In February 1935, Connie got a job in the Conservation Corps in Connecticut. He drove back in the Ford and went to work at Camp Filley on Route 9. In November 1935 he got another call, this time from the Torrington board of education. Fay Vincent had lasted less than 3 months as a teacher and coach, and his job was offered to Connie. It was time to come out of the woods. Connie, with some humorously barbed Irish blarney, told Fay in the passing of the torch/ football, "These aren't Yale students, you know." And Fay pointed out to Connie that he'd rather ref than coach these particular high school students.

Fay faded, and the THS show was Donahue's. (Right, a young Con- nie and Pete Dranginis, both THS teachers and coaches, at Fuessenich Park circa the late 1930s) "Mr. Vogel told me I'd be teaching classes and

coaching 3 sports. I asked him what kind of athletic budget I'd have, and he told me *none*! So we had more dances in the old bandbox (basement gym) than ever before. Tracey Garey had started the Athletic Association, and every student now paid 50¢ as a fundraiser. Charlie Thorpe got hit by a pitch in baseball and wound up in the hospital. The family needed help. I started an injury fund. Later on, of course, insurance came in."

In June 1936 he married Rose Brennan, and they had 2 sons: Tom (born 1939) and Dennis (1946). For awhile after he began teaching, Connie played summer baseball with the New City Boys Club, played some semi-pro, and some All-Torrington. But the athlete's part of his life was pretty much over. The injuries had been many; there was nothing left to prove. It was time.

Still, the excitement and sounds of athletics get into the blood. The strident caterwauling from fans. The desperate implorations from teammates. The obstreperous megaphonic cheers of, "DON-A-HUE!" It all becomes part of the Cretan labyrinth called self. The convolutions of the id through which past and present interweave into the "I."

(A faculty basketball team, circa 1940s. L-R: Connie Donahue, George Ganem, Pete Dranginis. Dog appears to be the best conditioned one.)

And so from 1935-'72 Connie Donahue stayed close to it all and coached. He coached baseball 1936-'72, basketball 1936-'68, and football 1936-'45 minus 1942. His 825 wins (825-519-5) underline the large portrait of him in the THS gymnasium, a gym which today bears his name (dedicated Jan. 5, 1990). He won a state title in baseball in 1939 and the basketball title in 1944 (Photo on right, Connie is flanked by his '44 Captain Ray Zucco on the left and his pivot man Bronc Callahan on the right). And Donahue won 21 NVL titles.

He has more personal awards than the entire coaching staff of THS past and present combined. Plaques wallpaper his tv room at home to include honors from the UConn Club, the Connecticut basketball officials, Watertown HS, Ansonia HS, the city of Torrington, etc. etc. Along with coaching, Connie taught for 35 years and was Athletic Director for 13; the jobs overlapped.

Connie and Jiggs Donahue formed a Recreation Committee that years ago merged with the Parks Department under the city charter. Connie started some of the summer Park and Rec programs, got businesses to donate uniforms, got high school players to go into the elementary schools to teach the youngster players, started block dances every Friday night, got 2 outdoor basketball courts open. And more. . .

His memory for names and his recall of events border on computeresque. He's honest and admitted that his worst coaching was done in football ("I was a lineman, so I didn't really know the inside stuff."). He was not above correcting a fallacy, explaining that *no*, he had not been an original member of the NCAA; UConn's Dee Rowe submitted his name in the early 1970s. And he doesn't duck questions. I asked him why in all his years there were no varsity female sports, when he himself remembered a varsity girls basketball team at THS around 1921. His answer: "All inquiries along those lines were referred to the female physical education teachers, and they wouldn't do it without pay. Besides, there was a lack of teams to play." It was a logical and forthright answer.

Connie Donahue is a good man, but even good men are not exempt from controversy, and Connie's had a bit. There was the time Huddie Richard from Richard's Sports Store was angry over his store's lack of athletic contracts with THS and Richard's charge of cronyism between Donahue and Lou Ganem from Sportsmen's Paradise. Nothing ever came of it. . . There was also the feeling in some quarters during the latter part of Connie Donahue's coaching career that his day had come-and-gone. But such feelings towards older coaches are not unusual, i.e. it's the inherent gap between the generations. . . Retrospection: Did Connie Donahue hang on to coaching too long? Was this the case of a self made man, who had risen through The Depression with a steely resolve, heat-tempered from digging ditches and cutting timber, refusing to let go? Thought: Maybe. Possibly. *But,* the bottom line is that no one in the public eye, certainly no coach, is exempt from criticism. And, moreover, Coach Donahue's teams kept winning, and winning, right up to his retirement. A *lot* of teens were better off for having the Donahue experience.

Connie Donahue had a nearly 50-year run with formal Torrington athletics. He told me the 1944 and '48 basketball teams were very fond memories for him. But that one of the teams he liked the most was also one of the worst, i.e. the 1965, 4-14 Raiders. He pointed out that one of the co-captains, Tom Higgins, is now a superintendent, and added proudly, "THAT was good coaching!"

Writer Harry Gallagher would agree. Gallagher in a 1976 article said, "To coach is to create, and it's a thing of which to be proud." Connie Donahue created, is rightfully proud, but his most ardent pride is neither for self nor for those framed accolades on his wall. It rather rests with the sportsmen he impacted: from those early Grove

Street tattered urchins with the taped ball, to 37 years of smartly outfitted THS squads. Ultimately, his pride, thoughts, and memories are with them all. . .

Connie could be fiery. Connie could be unsanded. But Connie in the final analysis is now an eight-decade old Vitascope, and a show unto himself. A big hearted Irishman who gave, and gave, and gave. It's the old parochial school lesson that it's more blessed to give than to receive.

And Connie has been blessed.

(Right, mid-1990s. Former Coach Donahue standing on the Torrington sidelines, still close to the game he loves, still the old warrior as he watches Coach Tony Turina's "modern day" Red Raiders compete. The white-haired octogenarian is probably remembering how it was. And perhaps missing calling the shots. *But,* he's also, no doubt, enjoying the *now* show in a gym that bears his name. And realizes that though his years are unmatched, a.k.a. The Golden Years of THS basketball, life goes on. Inextricably forward. The horizon and the future always just a heartbeat away. . .)

Images Of Connie Donahue Over The Decades With. . .

(The 1947-'48 THS basketball team arrives home from the New England tournament. Enthusiastic students greet players like Captain Ada Krulicki, John Cilfone, Rollie Spino, Andy Hricko, Gino Fabiaschi, et al.

(The 1964-'65 team, one of Coach Donahue's favorites. Front Row, L-R: Bobby Anzellotti, Terry Fogarty, Vin Avenia, Punky Amrich, Capt. Tom Higgins, Capt, Ralph Tedesco, Graham Martin, Jeff Pavan, Paul Geda. Second Row: Jerry Martin, Ed Schwartz, Joe Lefkowski, Lou Thuillard, Hugh Franklin, Bill Voght. Third Row: Doug Gyurko, Dick Cooke, Rich Ormsby, Joe Bianchi, Bill Scaia, Ron Romaniello, Manager Tom Bruni. Back Row: Coach Donahue, Manager Tom Barbero, Coach Lou Moscaritolo.)

(1957 w/Captains Ronnie Pace & Denny Summa)   ('72 w/Mark Fitzgerald)

(1961. Kneeling, L-R: Fran Andrews, Dick/Dirk Aube, Joe Germano, Rollie
Carlson. Standing: Walt Brothwell, Bob "Sal" Salinardi, Coach Donahue.)

(Late 1950s, THS Social Studies Dept. . . Seated, L-R: Marvin "Muff" Maskovsky, Eva Whitney, Rose Brennan, May Knight, Arlene Dullea. Standing: Charlie Duggan, Dave Bennett, C. Donahue, Pete Dranginis.)

(1966. Front Row, L-R: Manager Jim Benjamin, John Scarmana, Bob Miklos, Ken Hogan, Captains Ron Romaniello and Charlie Turina, Dane Peters, Buddy Burgess, Len Gerardi, Manager Ted Zielinski. Middle Row: Bruce Wilbur, Frank Bentley, John Farrington, John Copertino, Chris Germano, Len Lopardo, Dave Murelli. Back Row: Coach Moscaritolo, John Bado, Punky Amrich, Coach Donahue.)

(Above, 1962. Connie in his office at the old Church Street school busy with the paper-work part of being coach and athletic director. After this, his office till retirement would be at the "new" THS.)

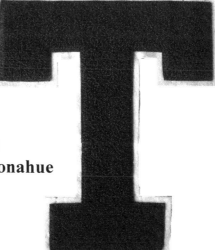

Rest In Peace
Cornelius "Connie" Donahue
1909 - 1998

(Moving out, moving in. On a crowded NYC sidewalk.)

Off To College
Goodbye And Keep Warm

(*The Torrington Voice*. October 23, 1997. There are keynote times in our lives, firsts that the majority of us share: entering kindergarten, winning a trophy, that first kiss, getting behind the wheel of a car, turning 21 and voting [and drinking], etc. But another benchmark is when one goes away from home for the first time, which for many is freshman year at college. It's a keystone *both* for the higher education initiate *and* the parents. . . Six months before I wrote this column I wrote one on the college acceptance wait. This October piece was a natural followup, one I thought a lot of people could relate to, and perhaps still can empathize with. . .)

Our older son left for college 8 weeks ago. And it's just starting to sink in that's he's gone, and he's *not* coming back. I don't mean that he'll never come home again, though he seems to have happily taken to the NYU/East Greenwich Village environ like the musical theater major he is, i.e. like some long-haired, sneakered, café au lait sipping, la bohème from the Washington Square cast of *Rent*. He'll come home for the big holidays; he's close enough for that. And I'll have to get off his waterbed when my back is bothering me when he does.

But he's gone, gone, gone as a Maynard G. Krebs, Jack Kerouac soul.

Simply put, he's left the dependent, schoolboy part of his life behind forever, i.e. the persona which toddled through the world on *our* purse strings of weekly allowance and on *our* dictates as overwatch parents. What he's graduated to are an escalating series of financial, social, and academic decisions that will be made by him. Decisions that will, cliché or not, affect the rest of his life.

Such a decisional and pivotal moment occurred last week when he checked in via his weekly phone call.

Son (excitedly): "Mom, Dad I got a part-time job at Urban Outfitters last week!" Us: "Oh, that's. . . good?" Dad: "Is the $1800 you earned last summer for spending money gone already?" Son: "It'll be gone by Christmas." Dad: "But that's over $100 a week!" Mom: "He's just exaggerating." Son: "No, I'm not. This isn't Torrington. You can't go out for coffee for a buck or two. And

41

beside, I thought you wanted me to get a job?" Mom: "I did, but your father never pushed it." Dad: "Your studies come first." Son: "I'm working hard." Dad: "I know you are. But if you have time to work, perhaps you should be getting some additional training. How about if I get the name of that uptown dance studio where Savion Glover trained? I heard it's reasonable." Son: "But I need the money. I need to work!" Mom: "We're proud you're working. We can talk more about it next time."

Momentary hesitations. Cool downs. Chat, chat, chat. Love re-affirmed all around. Goodbyes. Clicks.

One day you're telling your child what time to be home with the family car and to turn down the stereo. Eight weeks later child is telling you (past tense) that the gavel has come down on life-changing decisions, i.e. the torch has passed on, i.e. life goes on, oh-blah-dee-blah-dah. . . It's the child's infomercial to parents. The post be-home-by-twelve, no-phone-calls-after-ten world.

Surprisingly, it's the world we train our children for; yet, if you're like me, when child finally steps into the real mix, our reactions tend to be, "Whoa! *What's* going on here? Wasn't I just doling out your 50¢ allowance and buying you action figures like He-man and Shira?" It's easy to forget that *many* years have passed and the fact that conversations have subtly transmogrified over those years from the interrogative, "Dad, can I have a ride to Jaime's house?" To the declarative, "Oh that? It's an ear stud. Ten bucks a piercing. No risk of infection." End of discussion.

All at once it seems decisions are insular and non-negotiable with an undertone of, "Well, you might pay the tuition, and the room-and-board, and the phone bill, but that doesn't give you the right to tell me how to live my life." And parents, you may fight all this and bluster and fume and caterwaul. *But*, the evolution is going on, the rite-of-passage leapfrogging forward as inextricably as it went for you back in your bell bottom, Woodstock days.

It's a tough moment to realize that your own child has achieved quasi-independence that isn't far from complete. This is the young adult who as a baby used to fall asleep on your chest. This is the bambino whose toenails and fingernails you used to clip, whose hair you'd shampoo and blow dry. The knee-knocker who used to recite nursery rhymes for you, whose weekly highlight was family swim at the Y, followed by watching tv together. It was a big deal to walk to Doolittle's Bakery for a special treat, or to take an evening stroll to Yamin's for candy, always using the "secret shortcut" behind The

Good Life health food store. There were the moments of teaching swimming and diving. Of bike riding without training wheels. The water that was swallowed, the knees and elbows that were skinned hurt you almost as much. Sympathetic pain.

You worried over first steps and blocked off the stairs with an accordion-like gate. You fussed over the graduation from crib-to-regular-bed, and wondered if you were doing the right thing resorting to daycare. You took enough photos to qualify as an investor in Kodak, and lugged the suitcase-sized, shoulder-held camcorder to so many events that you developed a port list, all the while trying to freeze the evanescent passing of time. . . It didn't work. There came car driving lessons, of adjusting a prom-destined cummerbund, and finally of hugging an older teen in a maroon-and-white cap and gown clutching a THS diploma.

Who can say where the years went, only that they rolled by with an imperceptible passing. And now the child, our son, is gone, like all the generations of sons before him. He'll come home at Thanksgiving, but not really. His true home now is no longer in Torrington, or even in his poster-draped dorm room with email capability. His true home is now *self*, that place within the psyche that's furnished with all those qualities, values, and strengths that were hopefully instilled. It's a movable home, one he'll take with him wherever he goes.

I said farewell to our son 2 months ago thinking it was only temporary. Now I say farewell more permanently, though I can't say I'm easy about it. I fret over his welfare like Robert Frost fretted over the winter fate of an orchard he couldn't see. Frost told the orchard, "Good-bye, and keep cold," which is good advice for an orchard. My own advice is, "Goodbye, and keep warm." Be warm to yourself, son. And be warm to others. The rest, like Frost's orchard, has to fall to God.

43

Back To The Future
Torrington 1998

(*The Torrington Voice*. December 31, 1997. Another New Year's, another round of predictions for the upcoming year. One of these actually came true, to my immense astonishment. . . As in past re-publishings, names and the most dated speculations have been dropped, i.e. this *is* a humor break in the book and not an exhumation of the dead. . .)

Once again Torrington has whirled into that position on the space-time continuum in which our future spreads out before us like some great Cretan labyrinth. Only by staring into the emerald green depths of my 12-ounce Ballantine Ale, "America's Largest Selling Ale," does our common 1998 Torrington destiny reveal itself. . .

1. Having finally admitted women, the Elks will host it first ever all-Elk dance. It'll be held during mating season and will feature strange bellowing and much head butting, i.e. much like an evening Happy Hour.
2. *Bending to criticism that Winsted's Cinerom has more comfortable seats, our own multiplex near K-Mart will install seats featuring a variety of exotic positions and vibrating options.*
3. To boost the tourist trade, Christmas Village will stay open year round. It'll be explained to youngsters that Santa found the elderly housing here more affordable than at the North Pole and enjoyed the Meals-On-Wheels and Senior Center bingo.
4. *It'll be discovered that the reindeer at Christmas Village are the original ones from 1947 when all 8 sue for municipal pensions. An out-of-court settlement will be reached contingent upon them giving up the sleigh and moving to Maine. Or Litchfield.*
5. The showers at the Besse Pond Pool will be put on pay-for-view.
6. *Parking meters will be installed on Migeon Avenue. Confused convalescent home patients and the stiffs at Phalen's will have difficulty finding exact change.*
7. The Memorial Day parade will be baffled by the North End realignment and will wind up marching straight ahead into Zeller Tires, which specializes in alignments. While there, several WWII vets will be greased, oiled, and checked for proper inflation.

8. *The town historian will dispel rumors that John Brown as a youngster belonged to a gang at Highwood Apartments and that he bought an ax and broadsword at Morrison's.*

9. THS football will play several games under the lights until school officials realize the team looks better with the lights off.

10. *Several elderly will break out of the new assisted living facility on the Goshen Road. They'll be caught on nearby Lover's Lane illegally parking in wheelchairs and walkers.*

11. Local firefighters will come under criticism when they begin bungie-cord jumping off the new 100-foot ladder on the new $530,000 truck. The fire chief will defend it as, "Training that's necessary in case there's ever a fire in an elevator that keeps going up-and-down."

12. *The executive director of the Northwest "Y" will sue Big Y over the use of "Y" claiming that there is only one real "Y." Generously he'll offer the food store chain free use of "M," "C," or "A."*

13. As an experiment, the Sullivan Senior Center will switch its lunch menu to one high in antioxidants and human growth hormones. A beach will be built on the nearby Naugatuck River featuring nude sunbathing and skinny dipping.

14. *To celebrate the 50th anniversary of the Fuessenich Park lights, an evening celebration will be held. The 2 or 3 lights that still work will be turned on.*

15. The Firefighter's Museum will finally open and soon after will burn down. Firefighters, dizzy from all the bungie-cord jumping will mistakenly hose down The Place.

16. *A bike path will be constructed on the old Winsted Road railroad bed, though many will question why they are pedaling to Burrville.*

17. First Night will more accurately be renamed, "Last Night, First Morning, Morning After."

18. *An equitable deal will be struck with the 11 recipients of the heart-and-hypertension overpayment after lawyers plead, "Have a heart, just not theirs."*

19. Female city employees, who sued over sex discrimination in pay, will be appeased in 1998 when the City Council honors one as "Man Of The Year."

20. *And finally, Bentley will give up writing completely to devote his full-time energies to the seer producing qualities of Ballantine Ale. Torrington might not become a better place for this sacrifice, but c'est la ale.*

Long Live HANK Atop St. Francis

(The Torrington Voice. February 1999. File this under, truth is stranger than fiction, you can't make this stuff up. . . Out of all the things I've found amusing about Torrington over the decades, this has to be near the top of my list. AND, much to my delight and amusement, "HANK" is *still* there 17 years after I wrote this column. It's weather beaten these days, and not as *quite* as visible anymore. Still, it's an inspiration and template for all would-be pranksters. . .)

I'd just gotten out of my car last Monday in the back of the Torrington Historical Society, when I heard a voice yelling my name. Turned out it was one of the neighbors on nearby Alvord Street whose property abuts the Society's. "Look at the roof of St. Francis!" he was shouting. "Someone's written their name up there!"

I looked, but didn't see it, all the time wondering wondering how anyone could have climbed that steep pitch to spray paint a name. The neighbor directed me to move more to my left to avoid a tree and to focus on the upper left portion of the roof. . .

When I saw it, I lit up like an altar candle. There centered in a

background of powder blue slate tile was the word "HANK." Double take. Yes, HANK. The letters looked to be 6-8 feet high and were of the same blue slate as the rest of the roof, only a slightly darker hue than those tiles framing it.

I laughed. Studied it more. Then went on my way.

Later in a quiet moment the name HANK returned. Who was "Hank"? My best initial speculation said he was probably one of the roofers when St. Francis last got a new lid. He was, no doubt, a master craftsman who wanted to sign his work like any true artisan. Up until last year (1998) there had been a convent on that side of the church (On right, the St. Francis convent as it appeared in 1970). That convent had been there since 1893 and for a long, long time had obstructed a good view of the north side of the church's roof. And who tears down a convent? So Hank laid down his name in darker slate, feeling confident it'd never be discovered. Even his fellow roofers would have

been too close up to see it, i.e. it needed distance and even then a good angle, proper perspective, which the convent prevented. So Hank collected his pay check and left town feeling safe. Very safe. Only planes and God could see it, and if God cared about the signature, Hank probably rationalized that the deity would have knocked him off the roof after the letter "H."

Speculation-On-The-Speculation: Maybe Hank wasn't an artisan, but rather a POed former parochial school student looking for belated payback. Sort of a Blues Brother type who'd been smacked one too many times. Of course if retribution was the motivation for "HANK," I'm guessing he would've written something along the lines of #*! +# . . . But I'll let that thought go. . .

If it's true that Hank was a roofer, it'd be a simple matter for the church to check. Phone call to the roofing firm, yadayadaya, the firm checks its personnel files. After all, how many "Hanks" can there be in one small firm? Or "Henrys" which is considered the proper name for Hank? I've only known 5 Henry/Hanks in my entire life: Hank Milkowski, Hank Marchand, Hank Hoffman, Henry Herdt, and Henry Berglewicz. I carry a hankie, like a bit of hanky-panky, and got a hank of hair left (and a piece o' bone, and made a walkin' talkin' Honeycomb). . . And that's it for Hank/Henry in my own life.

I hope Hank escapes. He's already achieved folk hero status in my my mind along the lines of Robin Hood and DB Cooper. Of course, he may not be a roofer all. There are other possibilities. . . Perhaps it's a diabolical plot to get the church renamed Saint Hank's or Saint Henry's after the 12th century Roman Catholic saint and martyr. A renaming would certainly be cheaper than getting the roof tiles replaced. Thought: Possibly the conspirators behind any rededication plot are "Henrys" themselves. I counted 5 on one St. Francis donor list, and while 5 Henrys do not constitute a majority of parishioners, maybe this is some sort of small, secret power group along the lines of the Illuminati, Skull and Bones, Bilderberg Group, or the Torrington Parking Authority. . .

Possibly it's a clever scheme by the Main Street Action Team to drum up tourism. It's possible they plan to install some of those 50¢ viewing machines in front of the church and to hype the attraction on tv's *Unsolved Mysteries,* possibly making it a part of a religious series: The Shroud Of Turin, weeping/bleeding statues, the Fatima prophecies, Torrington's Hank. . . Or, perhaps the church itself is simply looking to recruit more members named Henry/Hank. Exactly why they would want to do this is beyond me, other than wanting to beef up their membership roster in the "H" category. . .

Could it be that it was the work of a celebrity, maybe Hank Aaron, Hank Snow, or Hank Stram looking for added publicity? They certainly have the $$$$ to pay off a roofer. I rule out Tom Hanks because of the "s" and the fact he would more likely deface the Warner or Cinerom.

Regardless of who the culprit is, I see this as a golden opportunity for St. Francis to make some money off the vandalism. The "H" could be changed to a "B" and the word "BANK" used to advertise the Torrington Savings Bank right across the street. Additional roof space could be leased out to advertise other Torrington businesses; after all, it's a *big* roof in a *prime* location. Might even put the ads in neon, and the lights could be kept on all night, i.e. downtown *is* zoned for business. I predict that advertising revenue would surpass the entire BINGO take from all years gone by.

All that aside, I personally plan on using "HANK" as a scapegoat for whatever goes wrong in my life. Example: Wife gets angry because I come in too late; it's Hank's fault. He made that new mosh pit on East Main too cool. Bought too many rounds of Ballantine Ale. . . And when asked who exactly this Hank is and where he can be reached, I'll just shrug and refer wifey to church officials. . .

There's no doubt that the mystery of HANK will close out the millennium and open the next. It'll never be solved. The best thing for St. Francis to do short of changing a lot of their prayers (Our Hank, who art in heaven, hallowed be your name Hank, etc.), would be to just add a "T" to the front and an "S" to the end, and make it "THANKS." Pointing skyward, it'll be oriented correctly for the Big Guy.

Hank himself, wherever he is, will have to miss it.

Rich Regis
A Profile In Courage

(The Register Citizen. May 7, 2006. Most Torringtonians, never met Rich Regis and, sadly, many these days never heard of him. Such is the nature of life lived outside the public eye. But, I feel safe in saying, most people know someone *like* him, i.e. someone who has had a life altering, catastrophic tragedy befall him/her.)

Rich Regis lives a quiet contemplative life these days. He has little choice. Since the beating he sustained in November 2004, he's been nearly totally paralyzed and wheelchair bound.

"I take life day-to-day now," he told me last week. "It's too hard to plan for the future. Things could change too drastically. I always depended on myself. Now, I have to put my trust in others."

Regis lives on a pretty back street in Torrington in the same brick cape he bought in 1990. He's not alone. There's the full-time caregiver Violetta from Lithuania who cooks, cleans, does the outside yard work, and sees to Regis's needs to include bathing, feeding, massaging, and exercising. She's an extroverted majordomo. There are also 3 cats, a Pekingese named Teddy, 4 large fish tanks with angel fish, parrot fish, etc. And there are parakeets who happily fill the house with singing. Rich's sister, Mary, has been an invaluable sibling, and she visits regularly.

Regis's special friend is Red, an old stray tabby that adopted him when the former Harwinton resident first moved in. Red divides his day between roaming outside and sitting on Regis's lap on a blanket so his claws don't dig in. Together they pass many hours in this position nodding off, watching television, and studying the fish. Red seldom changes position.

Rich Regis sits on a gel pad and will occasionally give the computer pads that wrap his head a tap to reposition the chair. He does this mainly when his muscles spasm, as his inert legs are prone to do.

"I can sleep comfortably in this chair for a couple of hours at a time," he said, but emphasized he does a lot more than just pass the time. "I taught Violetta to operate the computer, and we email my former workers, pay bills online: 5-to-10 minutes, all paid. We also perform Google searches (the latest in stem cell research, medical specialists in the area, etc.). I'm teaching her English, and I direct the cooking."

He paused. "It's easy to be down, negative. But it'd only make me sick. I focus on the positive things I can do."

Prior to the assault he led a hyperactive life.

The 46-year-old grew up in Harwinton. He was active in Troop 55 Boy Scouts and played on the Braves in Little League making the All-Star team. He laughed remembering the thrashing they received at the hands/bats of Torrington. At Lewis Mills he played for Leo Liddle in the band and went on to earn an Associates at Waterbury State Tech in chemical engineering.

"I always had a job," he said proudly.

He started at UniRoyal in Naugatuck, went nights to the University Of New Haven, and eventually completed his bachelor of science degree in chemistry with a specialty in synthetic organic chemistry. During his years at UniRoyal, Regis was awarded 6 patents that he co-invented.

"Financially, it was UniRoyal that benefitted," he said without bitterness.

When not working, he loved playing basketball, pitching horse-shoes, fishing for blues and stripers in Long Island Sound, scouring tag sales, working on old cars, and chopping, hauling, and splitting wood. Friends recalled that he seldom missed a clambake or pig roast.

"I had a lot of energy before this, he recalled. "Did a lot of multiple things at once. It was a huge change to have to sit still."

(Below, late 1990s, Rich Regis in better days. On left he kicks a 25-yard field goal on a Yale practice field. On right he uses picturesque form and follow through to put a flat spin on the horseshoe.)

Flashback: It was the weekend before Thanksgiving 2004, and Rich Regis was with his girlfriend Kelly Irene Donnelly at the West Cornwall estate of the elderly man whom she cared for. She was a nurse's assistant, ironically a certified caregiver. The couple had just been to her employer's 90th birthday party, had celebrated with a few drinks and dancing, and were now back in her quarters. It didn't take long. They were sitting on the bed, and there were jealous words from Donnelly regarding Regis's dancing with another woman. By her own admission later in the courtroom, Donnelly confessed to having a problem with alcohol. There was a long history when she drank of physical violence, to include several arrests. Regis knew nothing about his girlfriend's rap sheet prior to the trial, though he'd warned her before about pushing him. Regis is tall (6'4") but thin, while Donnelly is more compact. She was described by one reporter as "paunchy."

The attack came suddenly, without warning. She pushed him up against the rock-hard plaster wall, and he felt the shock wave travel down his spine in a wave of energy. When it hit his C-4 (the fourth vertebra down), he heard the bone break and felt the vertebrae above it collapse slowly downward like an accordion closing. Or the World Trade Center pancaking earthward. It gave him a squishy feeling that he compared to squeezing water from a sponge.

There was an emergency operation at St. Francis in Hartford. Then things got worse. Regis's body was jumping with electricity ("like I'd stuck a finger in a light socket"), lungs constantly filled with fluid ("I had breathing problems"), and a tube went up his nose and down his throat to drain the mucus. *No* anesthesia. His heart was arrhythmic, and he was wired up and told he'd need a pacemaker (never did). He had a chest tube for a partially collapsed lung, and respiratory therapists beat on his chest every 4 hours to dislodge mucus. Suction tubes went back down his throat. Then it was months of physical rehab accompanied by great pain and expense.

"I was lucky," Regis said looking back and meaning it. "They got to me right away."

These days Rich Regis is able to partially lift his left arm and his left fingers. But there's not enough strength to hold things or operate a remote or keyboard. He can lift one leg a smidge. From the chest up he moves normally. There *is* progress. But it's painstakingly slow.

I asked him if he thought there was a silver lining. He was deliberate in answering.

"I don't know if I believe there's a silver lining. It's all unbelievable. I wake up some mornings thinking I'll still be able to do what I did. It's what keeps me going. . . I like to dream about improving. I dream I'm healthy and about a lot of things I've done. My ID hasn't changed. I don't see myself as wheelchair bound. Some days I feel like I could lift myself up."

It's a rare courage Rich Regis has. Optimism in the face of paralysis. Christopher Reeve caliber courage.

People complain about the price of gas. Richard Regis would love to drive. Many folks whine if they have to mow the lawn, shovel snow, vacuum, do laundry, i.e. the mundane, *physical* things in life. Rich Regis would love to do any of that, and dreams about doing such ordinary work.

In adversity, people turn to God and ask, "Why me?" Rich Regis looks to heaven and thanks God for the day.

By odds Richard Regis should have died in West Cornwall. He doesn't know why he was spared, and neither do I. But he's a profile in courage, a lesson to us all. And maybe that's reason enough.

Postscript

Since I wrote this article 10 years ago, I've visited Rich many times in his Torrington home, though admittedly not as often as I should. He loves company, still is optimistic, still looks good, and still has a lively intellectual curiosity and an active sense of humor. He likes nothing better than to hear about what friends are doing and loves to smile and chuckle at life's foibles.

He's still wheelchair bound and has no use of his legs, though he's gained use of most of his fingers. He no longer uses his head to control his wheelchair but instead uses his thumbs to operate the motorized chair and the computer keyboard. He has DISH television and frequently watches sports and network programming. Combine this with the worldwide web, and Rich Regis is better informed than most of the people I know.

In many respects it's a full life, though a bit lonely with the cats, dog, parakeets, and all but one fish gone.

Violetta, his caregiver, is still with him. And they're now married. Other than skyping with her family back in Lithuania, Rich and this house with its manicured grounds (all improved through Violetta's efforts) are pretty much *her* world too. She loves to gamble on their computer (not for money) and recently split and stacked several cords of wood for next year's heating. She is a godsend, a strong woman who not-long-ago literally got in another man's face, nose-to-nose close, over the disrespect she perceived he showed Rich.

Rich's sister, Mary, is never far away. Like Violetta, she's a sweetheart.

Kelly Irene Donnelly served 11 years in prison and has been free for the past 1⅔ years. Rich doesn't know where she is and has no plans to ever contact her.

There is no bitterness in Richard Regis. There is only the *now*, and an undercurrent of hope that perhaps one day medical science will find a cure for his paralysis. Until then he takes life slowly and enjoys nothing more than visits from friends. And sitting outside in the sunshine.

(Everything Is Illuminated. Above, Rich on a long ago playing field,
back lit by sunlight and front lit by his eternally sunny spirit.)

Introduction
New Writings

(March 7, 2016. With spring less than 2 weeks away and nature ready to rejuvenate itself after a very mild winter, it's with a similar renewed sense of spirit that I begin to research and write a series of new features for this book. Because I'm putting a first ever emphasis on the THS sport of boys swimming, there's a personal element to the research that I'll be enjoying. . . I'd like to toss out a blanket, all-encompassing THANKS! to all those Torrington souls who gave their time and expertise to enrich this section. Without you, etc. etc. . . I'm going to begin this section with several short Torrington anecdotes and go on to more major features. . . A Special Thanks, as always, to **Paul Hultman** who recently drew, at my request, the new Joe Torrington caricatures below and to the right. **Paul Hultman** *is* as sharp, and as perceptive, as ever. As is Joe. . . And so without further. . .)

MORE
WRITINGS
AHEAD

The Coo-Coo Has Landed

(March 10, 2016. I like a good animal story, preferably one without death or permanent injury. *And* with a happy ending. This one occurred this past autumn. And while it's not especially emotional or unusual, it *is* mildly entertaining and does have a happy ending. Smiley emoticons all around. . .)

Think your Monday morning sucks? A real bummer? I come down to the kitchen this morning; wife's already gone to work. I clean out the cat litter and walk outside to the street and grab the morning newspaper. I settle in on a kitchen stool, pop open a diet ginger ale, scan the obits, and turn to the Word Jumble. NOTE: I never used to do the Word Jumble, and actually found it mildly annoying and akin to the buzzing of vuvuzelas at soccer games. But the languor of retirement in the last 2 years has elevated 4 jumbled words and a usually pun-oriented riddle to practically X-treme sports status.

I look at the first jumble: "doydl." I grab a pen. Channel 30 News is a low drone in the background. The cat is playing with something – a wadded up piece of paper? I'm about to fill in the boxes when. . . I hear this THUMP! I look around. The noise didn't come from Bob Maxon, NBC weatherman, i.e. he didn't keel over because of projected frost in the forecast. Did the cat knock over something? No, cat's now lying peacefully on a nearby rug hugging whatever it is she was batting around. Very cute.

I go to the back slider, cat follows. There on the concrete patio drain is a bird. Just sitting there. I tap on the glass; it doesn't move. I open the slider; it doesn't move. The eyes are alert, its head moving. But otherwise it's as inert as the nearby planter.

I close the slider and go back to the Word Jumble. I've seen downed birds before. Used to happen occasionally at our last house which sat on a hilltop and sported a lot of glass. Birds would see the sky's reflection in the UV-resistant, tinted Andersen panes. They'd continue to fly straight ahead thinking the glass was an extension of the sky, and. . . BAM! Sometimes they died; most of time they were only momentarily stunned and would eventually fly off again. Hopefully, with a lesson learned, though these are literally bird-brained creatures, so who knows. . .

Similarly, I think, this bird probably flew into the large pane of slider glass, is stunned, and now has a cat staring at it. Type of bird?

Coo-coo now. . .

Coo Coo Followup: Bird Daze. . . Around 11 a.m., after 4 hours of occasionally checking on the bird and noting that it was still sitting on the patio, though now by the fence about 4 feet from its original spot, I phone the Audubon Society in Sharon. I leave a message for Sunny Bettley, their wildlife rehabilitator.

A little time passes, and I have a gut feeling I'm not going to get a callback any time soon. I phone the North Torrington Veterinary Hospital run by the O'Gradys. This is a top notch facility with a caring and professional staff. . . The receptionist cannot be nicer. Tells me to bring in the bird, and if they cannot help it, they'll get it to a wildlife rehabilitator who can. No charge.

The bird is still immobile, though when I go to pick it up, it tries to fly away. But cannot. It's an easy matter to get it into a towel-lined box. Top is put on to give it a sense of safety and isolation. And 15 minutes later Coo Coo is in the professional hands of the NTVH pros.

Hopefully Coo Coo's recovery will be swift and complete.

All's well that ends well.

By-the-way, that first jumbled word was "oddly". . .

Oldies But Goodies At The Warner
Jack & Joan Be Nimble

(March 17, 2016. I've worked at many Warner shows in the last 6 years. While the work is usually routine, with the same sorts of problems and questions, every once in a while something occurs that's outside the Warner paradigm. This was one of those times.)

It was a great lineup featuring The Classics, The Drifters, Jay And The Americans, and Bobby Rydell. And the theater was nearly sold out. Around sixteen hundred white-haired, bald, and some-bent oldsters; many in walkers, wheelchairs, or wielding canes, crowded the main house and balcony. They applauded enthusiastically after each song. Some even used 21st century iPhones to relive and share their 20th century happiness. This Pop, Rock, & Doo Wopp Concert was senior heaven for them, i.e. the closest thing to nirvana on earth this side of Scarpelli's.

When Bobby Rydell did his final encore, and the predominantly senior crowd started to slowly file out after 2½ hours, I got a radio call to come to the lobby. . . My boss was standing near the concession stand and asked me to escort an elderly couple to their car. First time ever request. Unusual, but OK. Boss didn't say why, but I assumed they needed help walking and, moreover, might be afraid of getting mugged, though it's never happened to a Warner patron.

The man was thin and dignified with glasses, a mono-colored conservative shirt, and blazer. The woman was equally classy: good looking, well coifed, and sporting a very elegant dress. Capital Ritz. Most of our other patrons were dressed along the casual lines of going to the movies, a football game, or Senior Center line dancing. . . I offered my arm to the man because he looked more frail than his wife, though both seemed fine/healthy. His eyes went up, and he suggested his wife take it. I asked where they were parked and he said he thought out back. Near some wall.

We walked slowly but steadily to the side door, then down the alley to the back lot. I paused and asked where he thought his car was. He said he was near an important building and said again there was a wall. He said he didn't think they were supposed to park there. I pointed to nearby St. Peter's Church and asked if *that* was the building. He seemed confused, then looked towards East Main and said he thought they might be over that way. We walked south towards the large, high, wrought iron fence that marks our property boundary. There is no gate and no way over it, I realized, unless these seniors could pole vault. Or were hiding acetylene torches. . . To the right where the fence passes behind the Warner, it ends and segues to a 3-foot high concrete barrier, the type that transportation departments use on highways and interstates to close off lanes. It separates the Warner from The Nutmeg Conservatory parking lot.

"That's the wall!" the man said and I inwardly cringed. *They got over this?* I thought and asked, "Do you think you can get over it again? If not, you'll have to walk all the way around." I pointed off towards St. Peters. They said they could, and we threaded ourselves through the gauntlet of departing theater goers on this narrow side of the building.

Once at the barrier, I eased myself over and turned to help the woman. She waved me off, turned her back to the barrier, raised herself up on her tiptoes, put her keister on top, spun around, and stepped down on the other side alongside me. Bingo! Just like that. I was dumbfounded. She'd gotten over easier and more efficiently than I did. And in a fairly tight dress. The husband repeated the wife's maneuver and had there been scoring judges, 10s would now be flashing.

Their car was right there. I gave them directions to Route 8 South, and they varoomed off. I returned to the theater feeling that if they ever come back, perhaps I'll ask them to escort me to MY car. . .

Inflation Problems In Torrington

(March 23, 2016. Is there a direct relationship between getting older and doing stupid things? Judging by the Bentleys, I'd have to say yes. Emphatically. Undoubtedly.)

DUMMY AWARD
Winner

And The Dummy Award goes to. . . Backstory: Not long after we were married (about 100 years ago), Karen and I made the amazing discovery that we both did stupid things. Dummy things. Lots of them. And that's when we, by mutual consent, established The Dummy Award to be possessed AND displayed by whoever did the latest mindless faux pas. Over recent years it's pretty much sat on the shelf above my computer on a permanent basis.

Till now. . .

A few days ago the inflation sensor for one of my tires goes off. I determine it's the driver's side rear one, and Zeller's extracts a screw from it. No big deal. The very next day Karen tells me the inflation sensor on *her* car is on. I, once again, check the air pressure in all 4, drag out my air compressor, and inflate to proper PSI. I tell her the driver's side rear one was a wee bit down and to keep an eye on it. She drives around doing errands, goes to work, and the sensor's still on.

After work she goes to Zeller Tires. Like me she's there 75 minutes. A staple is removed. Labor cost $16. She comes home. Sensor's still on. She drives around some more. Sensor's still on. I check the PSI; it's fine. I tell her it's beyond me and to call the dealership. I add that her Fiat 500 is less than a year old and can't those Italians build a simple car like this one!? Must be the sensor. . .

She gets the business card from the owner's manual, and while she's at it decides to check the meaning of the dashboard icon one more time. . . Voila! Not the tire pressure at all. Nope. An early warning that within the next 500 miles or so the oil should be changed. . . Oil. *Not* air. . . And the new Dummy Award winner is. . . Merry Christmas, Karen.

Followup - This incident is so amusing to me I post it on my Facebook wall. My friends comment and laugh, and we all have a lot of amusement at wifey's expense. And that's it I figure. A few days later just before Christmas "young" Jim Zeller shows up at our door with a gift basket/ bucket to spread, as he says, some holiday "cheer." Wow. Totally unexpected. Not Zeller Tire's fault at all regarding the tire flub. BUT, this is what can happen when you deal with a wonderful, small town business like Zeller's. They've solved more car woes for us over the decades than I care to remember. . . The business certainly did *not* owe us thing. BUT a heartfelt thanks anyway to Jim and David Zeller and to *all* the Zellers. **Sidebar**: Note the tire inflation gauge (on right) taped to the side and the short message: "To check tire pressure only, not for use as a dipstick." And there you have it.

Business with a heart. *And* with an active sense of humor.

Postscript - Karen did not keep The Dummy Award long. It became mine again shortly after the holidays and is not likely to be transferred back to her anytime soon. . .

A Torrington Dental Story

(March 26, 2016. Does anyone enjoy going to the dentist? I don't, but only because I don't like giving up the time; and moreover, figure the news is likely to be bad, though it seldom is, i.e. I'm a flossing, gap scrubbing, tooth brushing fanatic. I know it's popular to

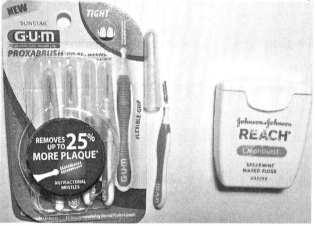

depict dentists as sadistic monsters along the lines of Steve Martin in *Little Shop Of Horrors* or WC Fields in *The Dentist*, which you can watch on YouTube. But, mine could not be nicer.)

So I go to my dentist this morning for ye olde 6 month teeth cleaning. I get there promptly at 8 (advantage = they can't be backed up to start the day), and I'm greeted by the dental hygienist who's bubbly and chipper and leads me to the room.

Sidebar: This is the 5th Torrington dentist I've had in my life. Doc Waldron was the first, a wonderful old gent. But he retired. Then I went to Izzy Temkin. Not a good match when 2 people are both politically inclined, disagree frequently, and one can't adequately respond because his mouth is stuffed with cotton. Next was Doug Traub till he retired. Then one who shall remain nameless. And now. . .

I hang my coat, sit in the chair, and the dentist herself appears and tells me she's going to give me novocaine. Says she's going to be going deep and if I experience any pain to let her know. I've never had my teeth cleaned by a dentist before, and never received novocaine for a cleaning. But I think, *OK. This is A-1 care.*

The assistant stuffs a suction tube in my mouth, and off the dentist goes: pulling, digging, and scraping. After around 30 minutes she tells me to take a break, the assistant hands me a magazine, and I think, *Damn, this is a helluva cleaning.*

Doc starts in again, and around 9 a.m. she finishes. Tells me I'm going to need a followup visit. Tells me not to floss between my lower rear teeth for a couple of days so the antibiotic can have a chance to work its full magic. I'm puzzled. Never got the usual buffing, or rinse and spit. In a tentative voice I say, This *was* my 6 month routine cleaning, wasn't it? She looks puzzled and says, No, it was a deep cleaning. . . You mean, I say, the one you wanted me to do a year ago to the tune of $400 - $500?. . . Yes, she says. . . But I told you, I counter a bit flustered, I *didn't* want you to do that. Add that this was only supposed to be a regular cheap-o cleaning.

She turns beet red. Looks at my chart. Says when my routine cleaning got changed (it was supposed to be next week), she got assigned to do it (no one else available), and she just assumed that I wanted the deep cleaning. Apologizes. Tells me it's on-the-house. Gets me a routine cleaning re-scheduled. Apologizes again. Smiles all around from the front desk staff.

After Thoughts: I guess I just saved a fortune. And I guess my gums and teeth are in better shape. *But* I can't feel my lower lip, and my teeth and gums are as sore as hell. AND, I have to go back. Hopefully, next time I'll get to rinse and spit. . .

After, After Thoughts: The antibiotic and deep clearning worked and the gap closed between my gum and tooth. I was happy with my sparkling clean and healthy teeth and gums. But felt guilty. Mistake or not, this was an hour of my dentist's time. An hour of professional, personal care. I knew she worked weekdays into the early evening and then had to go home and cook supper. I asked her if she liked eggplant parmesan. She did. Sidebar: I don't cook a lot of dishes, but that's one I've mastered: peel and slice around 2½-3 pounds of eggplant. Dip each slice in egg, then breadcrumbs, and fry. Layer with various cheeses and secret sauce. Bake. Total time with cleanup = 3 hours, approximately. *Not* that 3 hours of my amateur cooking time was remotely equal to an hour of my dentist's. *But* it was something. A goodwill gesture. And an expunging of guilt for me. . . I delivered the large warm pan of eggplant parm when she was about to leave work. And felt good about this visit to the dentist.

Sucking It Up In Torrington

(March 30, 2016. I do housework. At least some of it. I suppose it began when I was a sophomore at THS and one day got informed that from now on my brother and I would be washing-and-drying the nightly dishes/pot-and-pans. And doing the dusting and vacuuming. I balked at first. Told my parents it was woman's work. Ran away from home for 5 days rather than do it. *But*, quickly learned it was easier to help out than to survive in a cold November world. . . I now have many decades of practice. I don't mind doing laundry, washing dishes/pots-and-pans, or even cooking. *But*, I still don't like vacuuming. *And*, am still not very good at it. . .)

I suck. At vacuuming. Especially when the vacuum does not.

Explanation: So I'm dusting and vacuuming upstairs today in anticipation of boys coming home. My wife usually does it downstairs, and I usually do the upstairs. Why? Because she lives downstairs, I live upstairs, and that's the way we Bentleys roll. BUT also because I have many books, numerous wall hangings, and stacked shelves of bric-a-brac in my man-cave – all dust magnets – most of which she'd toss if she could. But she can't, i.e. there is no eminent domain she can invoke. So she prefers I clean up my own clutter.

I go over the rugs with the power attachment, then the floors, and lastly I'm using the brush attachment to get into all the nooks-and-crannies where the d-bunnies settle. I'm in the hallway and the vac unit suddenly drops in power, then loses it totally. It's a central vac system, so I go over to the wall outlet and jiggle the hose connection a few times. That's always worked in the past. But nothing. No suction. No noise.

I give wife a yell and she comes upstairs. I defer to her superior vac/suck knowledge and she repeats what I just did. Nothing. No suck. . . She goes down to the basement where the motor and collection canister are. I jiggle some more and she yells that the unit's going on-and-off in time with my jiggling. But still no suction on my end.

I look down the hose itself, then shake-and-shake it. Nothing falls out. We take it downstairs and try it in a different outlet. Voila! Full power. Enough to suck down a basketball. Enough to plant a hickey on Kenickie (a hickey from Kenickie is like a Hallmark card.) Wife gets out our small portable vac and I put the hose to the outlet hoping to dislodge anything that is stuck and blocking air flow. Nothing. Nada.

Wife gets on phone and calls Electrolux in Torrington. Gets forwarded to West Hartford. Is told it's $150 just to show up, and it goes up from there. She says she'll let them know. Calls Powell's Vacuum on East Main, despite her thinking that this business does not make house calls. Turns out that Powell's does, and will come for the same $150 just to show up. But first, the fellow sug- gests, Why don't you try a

wet-vac?. . . Good idea, I tell wife. Sidebar: I thought of the more powerful unit before, but was too lazy to haul it upstairs. Besides, I really didn't think it would work. . .

I haul the unit upstairs. Wrap a t-shirt around the end to seal the hose connection, hit the on-button, and put the plastic end against the outlet. Leave it there for long seconds. The seal is tight. Move it off-and-on hoping to shake loose any obstruction. The wet-vac is really sucking. This is good. High hopes. Wife finally hands me the regular hose. I stick it in. Nothing. Try again. Nothing. Damn.

I take the motor off the unit, attach the hose to the exhaust, wrap the t-shirt around the hose end, and this time when I turn it on, it's blowing, *not* sucking. REALLY *blowing*. A mighty wind.

We try the regular hose again, and voila! it's sucking. Fully suck-ing. Yahoo!. . .

Wife goes down to basement and looks in the collection canister. There she finds a dusting rag that wasn't there minutes before. Amazing. Apparently when I was vacuuming I passed over the rag I'd just used and sucked it up. The rag became the obstruction, a cloth barricade that had to be removed, blown out when sucked out didn't work.

Like I said, I suck at vacuuming. Hopefully the wife won't let me do it anymore.

The Old Fudge House
A Century-Plus Of Eerie Happenings

(April 1, 2016. Tales of ghosts in Torrington have abounded well into the 20th and 21st centuries. The Yankee Pedlar ghost of Alice Tryon Conley, wife of Frank Conley the builder and first owner of the hotel, is well documented and helped inspire the 2010 movie *The Innkeepers* with Kelly McGillis. The Warner Theater's infamous ghost, simply called Murph though it's more likely the departed spirit of retired merchant E. Frost Knapp who died in 1934 after a fall down the Warner's basement stairs, was the subject of a paranormal investigation in 2008. I once asked former town historian Ernie Ceder if there were any haunted houses in Torrington. He didn't answer right away, was obviously weighing the benefits/pitfalls of verifying rumor and scattered news reports, but eventually said, Yes, there are. . . He would *not* name specific locations or even general areas of our town. But, he did say in an August 2008 article in the Waterbury *Republican-American*, "We have ghost stories flopping all over the place," and added that he believed in *none* of them. . . Ceder's skepticism aside, my own research over the decades has uncovered the story of The Old Fudge House. References to the house have appeared here-and-there in newspaper brevities starting around 1883 and ending in 1955. What I present here is what I've been able to glean from newspaper archives, town records, the few Torringtonites who would go on record, as well as diaries, photo albums, and scrapbooks which I was given access to.)

Who hasn't felt the creepy sensation that he/she *isn't* alone even when no one else is around? Or, balked at descending into the basement, hesitated at coming into a dark house, jumped at unseen noises, found items moved, etc.? The Old Fudge House inspired all that, and generations of the house's owners experienced all the aforementioned, and more.

It all started during the French and Indian War. According to Samuel Orcutt in his *History Of Torrington, Connecticut* (published 1878), Private Jonah Fudge, born in 1737 in Torrington's western hills, around where Wright's Flea Market is today, enlisted in the Rogers' Rangers. He was said to be "hote of temper" and was eager to mix-it-up. The explanation given by Orcutt for Fudge's "steamy

68

bile" was that the woman he'd been in love with, Ophelia Wing, had died. Early town medical records list her cause of death as "drohwning," reportedly after throwing herself into a newly dug well near the Old Log Fort. Family records on ancestry.com claim that she'd grown despondent with "akute melancholia" when her father refused Fudge's marriage proposal to her and betrothed her to a much older farmer. Her last words were said to be, "A pox on King George and to all those who would deny a love that is true."

(Above, a granite marker in 2016 on the rise on Klug Hill Road just below Klug Farm. It was near here that Ophelia Wing took her life. According to colonial records, the fort cost townspeople "35 pounds, six shilling and six penc." Expensive, but also cheap given that Indian attacks were a very real concern in Torrington during the 1700s. And yet, after Wing's suicide not a single native American was ever seen again in this area. Many felt it was the curse, or *blessing*, of Ophelia's spirit.)

Orcutt reports that Fudge first saw action in the Second Battle Of The Snowshoes in 1758. It was a massacre that resulted in over 125 Rangers killed. Fifty survived, Fudge was among them. A year later Private Fudge participated in the Ranger raid on the Abenakis at Saint-Francis in Quebec, a battle made famous in the movie *Northwest Passage*. The Indian village was burned to the ground and over 30 women and children killed (movie aside, the Abenaki males were *not* in the village). Fudge was never the same again and was honorably discharged for reasons he would never talk about.

Returning to Torrington, he balked at living again at the family homestead and working the soil for a hardscrabble living. Instead he settled in the valley where the downtown Torrington Plaza is today. On a little knoll of land surrounded by tall and gloaming pine trees in the midst of Mast Swamp, he built a cabin and settled into a life of hunting, fishing, trapping, and occasional logging. It was a lonely existence, and the only human contact Jonah Fudge seemed to have was on his sporadic visits up the hill to Sheldon Tavern. The tavern was sited slightly west of where Klug's main barn is today, and a

granite marker (above) marks the exact spot.

That Jonah Fudge loved rum and hard cider was no secret to early Torringtonians. He would grow morose even after only light imbibing and was often seen, and heard, wandering and wailing near the Wing Farm, crying to the heavens for his Ophelia to return to him. Jonah Fudge's visits to the tavern grew less frequent as the years passed until he was a virtual recluse in the middle of Mast Swamp, his only company a wild dog which befriended him. Occasionally, workers from Amos Wilson's saw mill (around the site of the spillway on today's Prospect Street) would report Fudge's shadowy figure watching them from afar. Concerned townspeople tried to include Fudge in their socials, and ministers made frequent trips to his ramshackle hovel. But Jonah Fudge refused all overtures of outreach and friendship saying that he wasn't fit for human companionship. He asked only that when he died they bury him on his little knoll, and that if possible his dog be buried there too.

Jonah Fudge died at age 46 in 1783, right after word was reached in Torrington of the Treaty Of Paris and the end of the American Revolution. Several days of "heady intoxicacion" were given as the cause for his death, though he was also reportedly hit squarely in the chest by an errant firecracker lit off by celebrating village officials. Needless to say, Fudge had not been standing 400 feet back as required by today's statutes.

Pursuant to his wishes, Fudge was buried on his water locked knoll. Orcutt reports that for several days his dog lay grief stricken over his grave till "the flea-bitten mutt too passed away." Funds were raised for a limestone marker for the veteran. The limestone was poorly cut and within a few short decades the writing was illegible, the stone itself eventually crumbling and vanishing.

Over the succeeding years and decades, Mast Swamp was drained and the knoll and land passed through a succession of owners, none of whom ever kept it for long. Why the fast turnover? Local historians, such as Orcutt and Thompson, have speculated that it was for short term profit, i.e. with the valley reclaimed from the wetlands and the population ever growing, handsome profits could be easily and quickly realized for good, centrally located land. And there is some truth to that, though it is also true that the few small cabins that were built on the plot, after Fudge's hovel was razed, were abandoned not long after they were built. Why? Unsubstantiated rumors and town gossip claimed that Jonah Fudge's restless spirit and that of his dog scared off would-be settlers, though none of that speculation was ever officially verified. One incident that did make Bess and Merrill Bailey's Torrington trilogy concerned that of Polly Gilbert, a widow and the only single female who ever settled on the land. She claimed to family members that on several occasions her skirt flew up over her head as if blown by a "styff wind," though no such wind existed indoors, she pointed out. It gave her "extreme anxiety" though she also confessed to feeling "tingly thrills and shivers" which she said were "quite, quite pleasant." On other occasions she reported hearing a man crying, a dog barking, and a woman's blood curdling screams about King George, though in all cases no one else saw or heard a thing. Polly Gilbert finally moved after she claimed she saw an ectoplasmic phantom in green buckskin standing at the foot of her bed with his arms outstretched, beckoning her to come along, a bloody tomahawk in his belt. Her hair reportedly turned gray, then white and remained so till the day she died in 1870 despite local beauticians best efforts to color it.

In 1877, a substantial house was finally built on the property. Designed and built by industrialist Luther Hendey, it necessitated the leveling of the knoll and the digging of a full foundation. It was the first subsurface disturbance on the land which had hitherto supported only rustic, short term cabins. During the excavation, bones were disinterred and construction halted. A medical examination by long time Torrington physician Elias Pratt determined that the bones were those of an adult male and a dog. Whether or not it was Jonah Fudge, the doctor could not say. The remains were re-interred at Center Cemetery behind City Hall in an unmarked grave.

Construction on the large Victorian was completed in 1879. Its official address was 10 Treat Street, around where T.J. Maxx is today. It was considered one of the finest mansions in Wolcottville/ Torrington in its time. Luther Hendey spared no expense in either the construction or the furnishings, trying desperately to please his much younger wife, the former Abigail Israel (left) of Boston.

The Wolcottville Register made much of the engagement, marriage, honeymoon (the European Grand Tour), and the couple's settling down to life in the borough. Though not from this area, or ever having lived in a mid-sized town before, the young Miss Abby, as she was affectionately called, tried her best to fit in and was reportedly a friend to all: servants, industry leaders, politicians, merchants, neighbors, and even the occasional hobo looking for a handout.

From all outward appearances it was a happy union despite the 35 year age difference. The couple was blessed with five children, cared for a menagerie of cats and dogs, and maintained a chicken coop. For a decade or more the Hendeys seemed to have the idyllic existence.

It is not known the exact year strange occurrences began. The family was generally silent to outsiders about what went on within the walls at 10 Treat Street, as if by not admitting all was not prim-and-proper within their Victorian world, they could prevent it from getting any worse. Or at least not decrease real estate value.

(Below, the mansion circa 1890 with some of the Hendey children out front.)

Despite the unofficial Hendey silence, stories slowly emerged to the point that people began referring to the building as The Old Fudge House though there wasn't a living soul in the borough who remembered Jonah Fudge or Ophelia Wing. Much of the hearsay involved the usual paranormal activity: thumping in the night, footsteps, luminescent mists, hot and cold areas, flickering gas (and later electric) lights, misplaced objects, etc. i.e. nothing of a harmful nature. More mischievous than devilish. There was the time Miss Abby was late in getting dressed for the 1885 New Year's Ball at Achille Migeon's palatial estate, and she could not find her pearls. In frustration she berated the spirit, pleaded with him/it/them to *not* ruin her evening. And just as mysteriously as they had vanished, the pearls re-appeared – strung around her dog's neck. Another time during the couple's Sunday love making, at *the* climatic moment, a loud stentorian war whoop shook the bed and rattled the windows. It was alleged that Abigail Hendey was shaken to her core, and never again wanted to indulge Luther in his "often and lusty passions." Miss Abby held a seance in the bedroom the very next week, and eventually called in a Roman Catholic priest (though the family was Baptist) to perform an exorcism. Unfortunately, the paranormal activity did not stop entirely, though it *did* slacken off according to Abby's diary, which is on file at the Torrington Library. Church officials off-the-record blamed the exorcism's partial failure on the Hendeys for not keeping the Sabbath holy, and sex free. And for not tipping the priest 15-20% of the bill.

However mischievous and troubling the spirit might be, it always stayed away from the children. Was it protective of their innocence? If the ghost were Jonah Fudge, perhaps it was attempting to atone for the great wrong done to the Abenaki youth a century+ ago. Or, again like Fudge, maybe it just had no regard whatsoever for children and preferred buxomness females. It was said that Abigail Hendey was "very amply endowed," and because of her small feet always walked with "a forward pitch which threatened to topple her."

✢ ✢ ✢ ✢

By 1902 the Hendeys had had enough. The children were older, Luther was not doing well in his old age, and Abigail longed to return to Boston, to family, and to "a more cultured and spirit-free life." She told friends that just once she'd like to know the feeling of dressing and undressing alone. And not to worry about her skirt getting blown "bosom high." The Hendeys left Torrington and never returned.

(Right, a 1902 Torrington calendar from the business of C.H. Dougal on Main Street. The portrait was said to be inspired by Abigail Hendey. There were rumors at the time that pharmacist Charles Dougal was in love with Miss Abby, though whether the love was reciprocated, could neither be confirmed nor refuted. Douglas's ardent infatuation *might* have aided the Hendeys in their decision to leave town.)

The Victorian house was sold. Its reputation as The Old Fudge House no doubt hurt the selling price, which according to City Hall records was $5000, a small fraction of what it cost to build and furnish.

The new owner was a suffragette named Belle Barber. She was said to be a libertine, a believer in free love, and a user of opium. Rumors also persisted that there were rooms *and* ladies Belle rented out at an hourly rate. The bordello angle apparently did not sit well with the spirit of Jonah Fudge, and it was not long before the liberated woman was complaining to anyone who would listen that she'd been bamboozled in the real estate deal. That the house was uninhabitable. She cited instances of being groped and of having her private parts tickled. Of the garden hose soaking her before wrapping itself around her body and binding her to a hitching post.

She sold the house in 1903 for $3000 (taking a heady loss), stayed around town for less than a year before leaving. She was last heard of living in a sleepy Nevada hamlet which would become known in a few short decades simply as "Vegas."

The Old Fudge House went through a succession of owners over the next half century with those households having children and a quiet female in residence experiencing the least amount of ghostly troubles. One owner during the 1920s made it into a short-term boarding house for vaudevillians who performed at The Opera House on East Main and the Alhambra Theater (below) on South Main. The

Alhambra was close, 100 yards away, and the bohemian actors, actresses, and musicians who played its boards reported that The Fudge House was charming and conducive to artistic expression and inspiration. Unfortunately, when movies killed vaudeville, business at The Fudge died as well.

The house fell into heightening disrepair as none of the later 20th century owners could afford its upkeep or updating. The large house probably would have been turned into a group home or professional offices had it survived for another 20-30 years. But the Flood of 1955 heavily damaged it, and eventually it was razed along with the rest of the neighborhood to make way for the downtown Torrington Plaza.

In the final analysis there can be no doubt that at one time Torrington had a world class haunted house. A living reminder that "there are more things in heaven and earth (Horatio), /Than are dreamt of in your philosophy" - *Hamlet*. . . One old Torringtonian told me that the last owner of The Old Fudge House considered turning it into a Ghost Museum complete with exhibits and original artifacts. If that's true, it's a pity the Flood hit when it did. . . A retired carpenter also told me that the wood siding and interior paneling along with many of the large casement windows, and ornate plumbing and electrical fixtures were salvaged by a local contractor. The contractor later used the reclaimed materials to build "a craftsman style house somewhere in the city," according to the same carpenter who worked on the project but did not want his name associated with anything remotely supernatural.

Does such a house exist in Torrington? Is there a family today living within a sort of *new* Fudge House? Complete with Jonah Fudge, his dog, and the ghosts of spirits past?

If former town historian Ernie Ceder knew, he took that secret to the grave with him. And as far as anyone else goes, the living *and* the dead are saying nothing. . . as far as I know.

(Above, a photo allegedly taken in the non-modernized dining room of The Old Fudge House circa 1955 just weeks before the Flood hit. It seems to show the spirit of a colonial soldier – Jonah Fudge? – in buckskin stalking the premises. But *what* is he looking for? Peace? Lost love? His dog? Rum? Vintage nookie?. . .)

Delia Donne
A Renaissance Woman

(April 22, 2016. After the last article I took a few weeks off before starting this next feature. Spring had sprung, there were all the usual apres-winter jobs to attend to, and I needed them done-and-out-of-the-way, for the most part, before turning my full attention to researching and writing about a most unique woman: Delia Donne. Dee. Though both Delia and I had reservations about meeting and this writing project in general, I never doubted she was a person more than deserving of my full and best treatment. We had a history going back more than 25 years when she was mayor and I was giving her a very hard time, indeed, in the press. I'd like to thank Nancy

Sullivan Hodoski for acting as a liaison in arranging my initial meeting with Dee. Thanks also to Dee's daughter Joanne for her willingness to identify people in photos and fill in gaps. And finally I'd like to thank Delia herself for being gracious throughout the interview process and phone calls. The past may not be forgotten. But it certainly has lost its bite between us. . . It was nice to talk with you, Dee. A pleasant pleasure indeed.)

Delia Donne. A dame. A tough Italian businesswoman. A strong willed politician. *BUT*, also a smart, savvy thinker and organizer. A fiercely loyal friend. A person of boundless energy and someone who embraced the best of the American can-do spirit during her most active years.

Delia Donne was the first female mayor in Torrington. If she accomplished nothing else in her career, *that* would still be a major benchmark both for her and the town. BUT, there was a lot more. She came out of the Depression years and went to work to help support the family. She eventually managed 2 businesses, started her own, expanded it, rose through the political ranks, led organizations, volunteered – all while building a house/home, raising 2 children, and constantly relishing a challenge. She rose to every occasion, did not let temporary failures stop her, and constantly surpassed others' expectations for her.

❖ ❖ ❖ ❖

Delia Donne was born Delia Rose Paniatti in 1930 in Stamford, Connecticut. While she was still a toddler the family moved to Sharon Avenue in Torrington. Her father, Louis (actually Luigi), worked for DeMichael's Construction on High Street, but tragedy struck after only a few short years. Delia was 4-years-old when there was a car accident, and Louis died of a brain injury. The Depression years, which were tough for every Torrington family, now became tougher for the Paniattis.

The family consisted of mother Angela (center), sister Flora (on right), and the 5 year younger "baby" of the family Delia (on left). There had been a brother, but he died in infancy. The 3 Paniattis were now living on French Street, and were forced to take in boarders. In addition the mother Angela did the laundry for well off families, and the family maintained a small garden. There wasn't enough land to support much more than a supplemental crop. There were no pets. When she was 11, Delia delivered groceries in a wicker basket for the neighborhood grocery store, Trinchero's, on Lafayette. She was paid 25¢ an hour.

"There were good years, and bad years," Delia told me recently. She remembered wearing hand-me-downs from the neighbors and regularly walking to a garage behind City Hall to pick up government food allotments. "There was no social security in those days," she said, but remembered the generosity of an uncle who bought the family a red wagon so Delia and her sister Flora could have an easier time bringing home the state handout. Easier, that is, till the sisters hit the steep hill of Summer Street. "One pushed, the other pulled," Dee remembered and added that the allotments included prunes, apricots, and large cans of various food stuff. She well remembered eating chicken and liking it, till she later found out that what her mother had been calling chicken was, in fact, rabbit. "A lot of people had rabbits, she said. She also gave her mother great credit for cooking rabbit, and polenta that was "to die for." She remembered eating a great deal of ravioli that her mother made from top-round beef that she got from the butcher. Delia said that her mother was a terrific cook and that "food was important; everything was homemade."

That love of food and culinary adeptness would be passed onto Delia, who was a quick study and a natural talent in the kitchen. Her skills would prove invaluable in a few short decades. But, it wasn't time yet.

"We played duck-the-rock (also known as duck-on-a-rock), and sometimes we played it under the streetlights," Dee recalled. Sidebar: There isn't anything more basic, cheaper, or more character building than tossing a rock at another rock and having one person guard it and weather an onslaught of stones. Hones guts, speed, and nerve. It was a popular game in the neighborhood, a neighborhood where Delia had many friends: Glen, Mary Ann, Elaine, et al. Even aside from informal games, Dee was active. At Southwest School she was a majorette. She recalled needing a certain kind of shoe to complete the uniform of a baton twirler, and remembered that Alice Fabro generously bought a pair for her. She was the kind of child that people wanted to encourage.

Delia matriculated at THS near the end of WWII, but dropped out after 2 years. "I got tired of being on welfare and wearing hand-me-downs," she honestly admitted. (NOTE: Delia would eventually go back and earn her diploma.) She got a job babysitting on Irving Avenue, but it was not much money for the long daily walk back-and-forth between the lower East Side and French Street. She next landed a job at Fitzgerald's in the North End behind McDonald's where K-Mart used to be. "I earned $30-40 a week and thought it was a lot. I turned it all over (to mom). I worked for John Weber. It was easy office work. I stayed there for a couple of years, then went to work at The Register." Delia said she operated a teletype machine, and I asked how good a typist she was. "You learn anything when you have to make a living," she accurately appraised. She liked working at The Register, they liked her, but after a few years mother Angela got sick and Delia had to stay home and take care of her. She admitted that families stuck together back then, often lived together, and were more sociable towards each other.

And what was Delia's social life like as a young woman in post-war Torrington? "We went to dances at the White Eagle, the Polish National Home (next to the firehouse), and the Piemontese Club on Chestnut Avenue." She remembered being "not bad" at the polka but gave her sister Flora credit for being better. She talked about long tables and rolling dough for ravioli and gnocchi.

Delia remembered walking past the American Brass at night and "the fires going full blast. Guys would be sitting by the grate to keep cool and would tell me I shouldn't be walking alone. But we survived it all."

Survival. Overcoming life's natural toughness and doing it with a smile and bouncy spirit. It was the motif of Delia's life.

A major benchmark entered her life in 1950 with the arrival of Louis Gath Donne, a mason working for Bonvicini Building. They met at the White Eagle and were married (above) in November 1950.

It was a large wedding in the grandest of tradition. Reverend William Botticelli performed the double ring ceremony at St. Peter's. Miss Clair DeMichiel sang; Mrs. Sophie Ganem created the wedding cake. Dee was fabulously glamorous in her gown of white Renaissance lace over satin. Her sister Flora (now) Nebiolo was matron of honor. Bridesmaids were Miss Marilyn Chadwich and Miss Helen DiNoia. The wedding dinner was at Wolcott Restaurant, the reception in the upper St. Peter's Hall. The honeymoon took in NYC, Washington, and Virginia, though Dee looking back remembered that the weather was so bad that the newlyweds could not get beyond Waterbury the first night, the wind so strong that the hotel flagpole was bent nearly to the ground.

Married life accelerated things, if that was possible, for the 20-year-old Delia. In 1951 son Louis (Chip) was born; followed a few short years later by daughter Joanne. The family moved from French Street to Roosevelt Avenue. Then Louis Sr. built a brick house on 176 Highland Avenue for them, i.e. he was a good match for the energy and drive of his wife. During the children's very earliest years Delia didn't work but concentrated raising a family, e.g. the kids came home for lunch and in the grand food tradition of the Paniatti kitchen, got a homemade one. Around 1959, Delia returned to work and quickly rose to become manager of the S&H Green Stamp Redemption Center (below).

(L-R: Clara Grossetti, Rena Spadaccini, Delia Donne, Carolyn Conti Mazzaarelli, unknown.)

Delia worked there for 8 years.

In November 1967 Harold Reibman announced, "Mrs. Louis Donne has been appointed manager of the soon-to-open Gazebo in the Torrington Shopping Parkade." Gazebo, which was in the back of the Winsted Road Parkade where Richman's and the cinema were, was owned by Jim Marine (Quality Hat) and Harold Reibman (Reibman's). Gazebo was described as an apparel shop for both young women and men. Nancy Sullivan Hodoski was one of the early teen employees. Regarding her boss Delia Donne, she said: "Dee threw me a lot of responsibility. She believed in me. We went on buying trips together. I don't know if Dee would realize it, but she was fighting to succeed in a man's world." A fighter *and* a busy woman. At the time Delia was also vice president of Altrusa Club, hospitality chairperson of the Augustinian Recollect Guild, a director of the Chamber Of Commerce, member of the Columbiettes, and a past president of the Piemontese Auxilary. She clearly was a person whose energy was only rivaled by her skill in directing it to worthy causes.

Always a fashionable woman, Delia Donne kept abreast of the latest trends and happily managed Gazebo for 2 years before deciding she wanted to go forward on her own. Her love of food, culinary adeptness, and natural talent in the kitchen now rose to the forefront, and in October 1969 she opened Dee's Coffee Shop and Delicatessen on lower Water Street next door to Laraia's on the north side of Water. It had formerly been Fitzsimons Deli.

She had no food service experience. It was a gutsy move.

"I bought the business for $5000," Dee remembered. "Clara (Grossetti), Von (Rusckowski), and I did the cooking."

By all accounts it was a homey atmosphere. Initially there was only one room and it functioned as a deli. It wasn't long before a wall was knocked down and Dee's expanded into the space next door to create a formal dining area. Long time Fitzsimons waitress, the always spunky Carole Bielik, humorously told me, "Dee bought me, when she bought the place." Bielik had been a waitress for the previous owner for 6-7 years and her presence brought a sense of continuity and experience. Dee's daughter Joanne joined the staff, and she waited tables starting her sophomore year at THS. The other seminal employee was Ronnie McManus. The business soon established itself as a hot spot for good food and lively conversation.

A regular clientele established itself. Carole Bielik: "Everyone knew everyone. It was like a family. At times there were lines halfway up Water Street."

(Right, Water St. in 1968 the year before Dee's was established.)

"The Torrington Company employees came in first," Delia said. "We saved a big round table for them. At 1 p.m. the table was taken over by the merchants. Slowly more politicians came in: Eric Chadwick, Izzy Temkin."

The round table was by the front window and at various times during the day sported local notables such as Fred Bruni, Joe Ruwet, the Mazzarellis, et. al. See and be seen. Bielik: "I'd go over to them and say, 'What problem of the world are you solving today?' "

Bielik was the proverbial wisecracking, heart-of-gold waitress. She tells the story how a fellow came in one time, ran up a big tab, then confessed he had no money. Offered to wash dishes. "I told him to pay when he could, and I paid his bill. He left. It wasn't until the next day when the newspaper came out that we discovered he was a reporter, and it was all for a news story." Bielik said he *did* come back and pay.

Generosity was a cornerstone at Dee's. Dee herself reportedly did a lot for people who were down-and-out such as giving away food. There was not only this generosity with her own bread-n-butter, so to speak, but also the generosity of spirit and emotional outreach. Employees dressed for Halloween. At Christmas the lyrics to an

Italian holiday song were passed out, and everyone sang. The tree outside by the curb was decorated with Easter eggs. The kids from LARC would come in with their checks and the staff would take them under wing.

Delia told a reporter in 1983, "People come to us with problems all the time. Sometimes they need advice about their marriage. Sometimes it's teenagers with problems. And other times it's drinking problems or drugs. But they know they can knock on the door, and I'll be here to help out. The way I see it, that is just one function of running a small town restaurant."

Outreach. Carole Bielik smiles and recounts how one time Dee took her to the Torrington Police Department jail because one of the restaurant employees had run afoul of the law. "We brought a cupcake and candle, and sang Happy Birthday to him," she smilingly remembered.

(Above Dee's staff circa 1969-'70. Front Row, L-R: Peggy Chiarito, Unknown. Second Row: Nancy Klens, Carole Bielik, Delia Donne. Third Row: Mary Ruskowski, Von Rusckowski, Clara Grossetti. Back Row: Billy Celadon, Joanne Donne.)

Outreach and food, food and more food. The people must be fed. Delia herself recounted how at times after catering late, they'd be sitting on the sidewalk in front of the restaurant eating and the police would come by. "We'd offer them food," she said, "and they'd have a little." Neither late hours nor weather deterred Dee's Deli from serving. Bielik: "There was a blizzard. I was home, and Dee phoned. Told me I had to come in. 'How am I going to get there?' I asked her. She sent Junior Powell with his garbage truck to pick me up."

Of course, at the heart of any restaurant is the food. Delia said the menu featured, among other wonderful things, "great homemade soup." Carole Bielik remembered the macaroni-and-cheese and Von's "famous" bread pudding but noted sadly that Von would never give out the recipe and "took it to the grave with her." As regards pudding, there was a fine assortment: bread, chocolate, tapioca, Indian, and grapenut – each 60¢ a serving. Cheap by today's stan-dards, inexpensive then too. Reportedly Dee never went up much on the prices over the 18 years her restaurant was in business. It was considered a place for the working person and an effort was made to keep it as such. (Opposite, p. 2 of Dee's four page menu.):

Though Dee's was an eating and meeting place for the common folk, a number of political celebrities stopped in over the years including Ella Grasso, Bella Abzug, and Barbara Bush. Celebrity or hoi polloi, the wait staff handled all with equal aplomb. Dee set the example, and it was an experienced and sharp crew that followed. Sidebar: Probably no one was more experienced in food service than Von Rusckowski who waitressed at such places as TCC, Litchfield Farm Shop, and Beverly's Roaring Twenties over the years. She was still serving diners well into her late 80s at DiFranco's in Litchfield before dying at 93 in

2014. Like Dee she followed the Torrington scene acutely and had a business card (above) made up to that effect. She was by her own

self proclamation, "The eyes and ears of metro Torrington." She had a great sense of humor.

appetizers

ANTIPASTO		HOME MADE SOUP OF THE DAY	
Small ...... .95	Large 1.35	Cup ...... .35	Bowl ...... .65
CHEF SALAD 2.25		CLAM CHOWDER (Friday only)	
French or Russian Dressing ...... .25 (extra)		Cup ...... .55	Bowl ...... .90

hearty sandwiches

served on your choice of bread

Bacon Burger ...... .95		Ham & Cheese 1.00	
Baked Ham ...... .95		Ham Salad ...... .75	
Bologna ...... .75		Hot Dog ...... .65	
B.L.T. ...... .90		Liverwurst ...... .80	
Cheeseburger ...... .90		Meatball ...... .85	
Chicken Salad ...... .90		Meatloaf ...... .85	
Corn Beef 1.25		Pastrami 1.00	
Eggplant 1.00		Peanut Butter & Jelly ...... .60	
Egg Salad ...... .75		Pepper Burger ...... .95	
Fishwich ...... .95		Reubens (Corn Beef, Cheese & Kraut) 1.75	
Fresh Turkey 1.25		Roast Beef (home cooked) 1.25	
Friday Burger (Fish, Cheese, Coleslaw, on bun ...... .95		Salami ...... .85	
Grilled Cheese ...... .75		Swiss Cheese ...... .80	
Grilled Cheese & Bacon ...... .90		Tunacheesewich (Grilled Cheese & Tuna) 1.00	
Grilled Cheese & Ham ...... .90		Tuna Salad ...... .90	
Grilled Cheese & Tomato ...... .85		Lobster Roll (when available) 1.75	
Hamburger ...... .80		Veal Loaf ...... .75	
Ham Melt Burger (with Cheese on Bun) ...... .75			

On all above sandwiches the following items are extra

Lettuce ...... .10   Cheese ...... .10   Tomato ...... .10   Toast ...... .10

Pepper ...... .15   Onion ...... .10   Bacon Strip ...... .15

dee's delicious club sandwiches

All served with Bacon, Lettuce, Tomato, and French Fries

Turkey ...... 2.15   Hamburger ...... 2.15   Roast Beef 2.15

Cheeseburger ...... 2.15   Ham & Cheese 2.15

bulky grinders

Salami or Ham 1.55		Sausage & Peppers 1.60	
Roast Beef 1.75		Meatloaf 1.55	
Hot Meatball 1.55		Hot Pastrami with Cheese 1.65	
Hot Eggplant 1.65		Combination (Ham & Salami) 1.55	
Corn Beef 1.75		Tuna 1.65	
Cheeseburger 1.90			

side orders

Salads are also available by the pound to enjoy at home

Cottage Cheese ...... .45	Potato Salad ...... .45	Cole Slaw ...... .45	Macaroni Salad ...... .45
Jello ...... .45	French Fries ...... .50	Onion Rings ...... .60	Large Toss Salad ...... .65
Small Toss Salad ...... .45	(French or Russian Dressing ...... .15 extra)		

Miscellaneous Local Memories Of Dee's Deli:

Ray Carcano: "Father Ron Genua used to drag some of the St Peters kids there for coffee/sodas/lunch after he put us to work on specific CYO and other parish events. That's where I learned to drink black coffee."

Ed Pescatore: "I don't have much for a memory. I was just a kid, but I remember going there with my grandfather."

Lucille Fines: "I remember going to her restaurant on Water Street. The food was great, but what I remember most was Dee walking around, greeting everyone, and making sure everything was okay. She was so personable, and she made us always feel welcomed! That impressed me at my young age. I also attended a bridal shower for my girlfriend there. It was a great place!"

Tricia Frazier: "Dee wore her hair up in a chignon with a net over it. My mom admired her updo so much, she had her hair done the same way. Dee would come around and talk to her customers. As a young girl, I admired her!"

John Todor: "One of us working at Howard's in the 60s made a breakfast run, and sometimes a lunch run, out the back door to Dee's every day. The pastries were great. Always a large order from Howard's."

Daryle Abeling: "Dee was always on hand to greet her customers and make sure we were happy with our order. I recall the best 'mac & cheese' ever and lemon meringue pie to die for! Great lady."

Deb Gath: "I was going to hairdressing school upstairs at the time (Torrington Beauty Academy). I used to go to Dee's for lunch everyday. Everyone used to stop in, and she would always come out and speak. You could always hear her because Delia had that deep raspy voice. She would joke and speak with everyone. I remember Dee sitting on laps joking with the customers often! The food was good; the servers were like family."

Carl Hewitt: Several officials and I from TPD made Dee's a regular for lunch just about every day of the week. Unless we were on some kind of case, Doc Antonelli, DePretis, Columbia, Joe Hayes, and I ate there faithfully. The food was always good, the regulars fun to chat with during lunch. Dee and Carol came around to talk and joke with us and discuss politics. Dee was a wonderful hostess, always with a smile and kind words for everyone surrounding her."

Emily Decker: "In those years I was an employee and then store manager of The Singer Co. store on the corner of Main and Water, and Dee was our next door neighbor. Ate lunch there every day. She couldn't do enough for her customers. Great food and great ladies working there. Dee, Veronica and Carol are the ones I remember. I also remember Dee was active in helping to save the Warner."

Bill Celadon: "The year was 1969, no later than '70. I was a custodian at St. Peter's for about a year and would pass through Mertz twice a day on my way to the original small Dee's, now maybe Pure Silver. Just working at the church afforded me a free coffee. I could hob-nob with the local celebs, clergy, and businessmen including Dave Jacobson, owner of the Warner at that time. I would stretch my break time often, and I became one of the gang I suppose (Note: Bill Celadon is in the staff photo on p. 85). I was very sweet on 16-year-old Joanne, and still carry a torch. Dee liked me."

(Below, Dee and daughter Joanne at the counter.)

Time does not stand still, and neither did Delia Donne. In the winter of 1978 she made the decision to move her restaurant across the street into the larger, former Quality Hat space in the Lilly Building. By mid-April the move was complete. Dee's could now accommodate 120 diners, breakfast through dinner.

Three years later, in 1981, Dee and daughter Joanne (Bielawski, at the time) went into partnership. It was a good match. Joanne told a *Litchfield County Times* reporter: "We get along very well. . . I'm the boss, and she listens." Such tongue-in-cheek humor assured that Delia's nervous energy (by her own admission) and Joanne's calm,organizational skills (as mom attributed to her) did not clash. Their roles were clearly defined, and maintained. Dee handled the catering, Joanne the daily running of the restaurant.

As the years had rolled along, Delia had become more-and-more enamored with politics. It was a natural evolution with her restaurant being the informal headquarters for local politicos. In 1971 and '73 she ran as a Republican for the City Council and was defeated both times. In 1975 she ran as an independent, and again was defeated. A weaker willed, less focused person would have given up. Dee was neither. She continued to work long hours at the restaurant, and bided her "free" time by joining the Civil Service Commission, volunteering at FISH, working for the hospice team at the Brooker Memorial, and serving on the Nutmeg Ballet's advisory board.

In 1983 she ran a 4th time, and this time won! Not only did Delia win, but she was the top Republican vote getter. Prior to the election she told a reporter: "I don't think the town was ready for a woman before. I just feel maybe this is my time. I feel the people's reaction to me has been different this time."

The Delia Donne express train was on the move, and the next dozen years would be hers. In 1985 she got the GOP's mayoral nomination and went on to defeat Peter Landucci in the general election by over 400 votes. In 1987 she beat Harry Hamzy by nearly 4500.

(Above and left, political giveaways: a keychain, refrigerator magnet and letter opener)

Sidebar: As Dee was winning victories, and giving Torrington her full attention, daughter Joann, now a mother herself, decided that she needed more flex time. In 1987 she sold the business and started her own real estate agency, a venture in which she could set her hours. Sidebar 2: Carole Bielik would once again go along with the sale, and now worked for Firori's.

In 1989 and 1991 Dee narrowly defeated JoAnn Ryan: the first time by 44 votes; the second time by 245. In 1993 she crushed Jack Dillon by over 4300 votes. Not only was Delia the first female mayor in Torrington's history, but she was a major hit and held that position for a decade (1985-'95), 5 consecutive victories.

In the contentious 1995 campaign, much was made of the old political saw that it was, "Time for a change." Delia was resoundingly beaten by Mary Jane Gryniuk by almost 2000 votes. Delia came back in 1999 but again was defeated by Gryniuk, this time by a little over 400.

An era was over.

Delia was gone from the political scene, but *not* forgotten. Accomplishments under her administration were many. Bridges were

(Above, Delia and her husband Louis at her 1993 mayoral swearing-in ceremony.)

repaired, the Industrial Park filled, the garbage Transfer Station opened, sewer lines replaced, the sewage plant itself upgraded. The Donne years oversaw renovation of the TPD headquarters, expanded the Sullivan Senior Center, saw completion of the Torrington Commons (Stop & Shop), and obtained grant money for many *many* projects including the Vito Colangelo Sports Complex, elderly housing rehabilitation, and downtown revitalization. Laurence Square was reconfigured, a new middle school approved and started, and the old Wetmore School demolished and the new Vogel-Wetmore School complex slated to open soon.

That there were critics, myself included, over some of Mayor Donne's decisions goes without saying. Controversy is an unavoidable byproduct of politics especially when one is seated where the buck stops, i.e. in the mayor's office. Delia accepted it. Told me recently that politics is a big person's game, as is news reporting.

That Delia succeeded on the street/personal level is unarguable. Success in politics in small cities like Torrington depends on being responsive to the nuts-and-bolts whims and requests of the electorate. This person is getting a flooded basement because of street run-off, this one wants a streetlight, this one is unhappy about the potholes on his/her street, etc. Dee responded very well to individual gripes and requests because, I think, she knew it was good politics. But more importantly because she genuinely liked people. Liked helping them with their needs and easing their troubles like the good Italian matriarch she was. And still is.

Regarding her interacting on a personal level, Eileen M. Ryan remembered that, "Dee invited my Mom, Mary O'Reilly Ryan, to be Lord Mayor of Torrington for St. Patrick's Day during Dee's first year as mayor. Mom loved it! We used to have 'open house' every St. Patrick's Day. Dee would come, have a corned beef sandwich, a beer, and enjoy the evening." . . . Democrat Bill Celadon admitted to voting for Dee "many times." Told me humorously, "My vote was bought with (free) coffee."

Life post-City Hall was less hectic for Delia but was still filled with worthwhile activities. She became a certified justice-of-the-peace and performed weddings. Diane Marie Finello Thompson said, "Dee performed my wedding ceremony on Bishop Donnelly softball field. It ended up on the news and front page of *The Register*."

Delia was named chairperson one year for the American Heart Association's "Hearts In Bloom" campaign. She became the first woman inducted into the Torrington chapter of UNICO. She took the post of director of operations at Wisdom House in Litchfield. She had her own Laurel Cablevision 5 program called "Cookin' With

Wisdom." On that show she shared some of her own homemade recipes such as marinara sauce and also featured non-celebrity guest cooks who shared their own "quick and easy dishes." And she wrote an occasional letter-to-the-editor, still following Torrington's political scene.

Delia Donne's legacy to our city is that of a Renaissance woman, one who had a surfeit of energy and drive. And who never let failure or obstacles get the better of her for long. She had to drop out of THS to help support the family, yet while still a businesswoman and homemaker, she successfully went back and completed her GED in 1975. She was a working mom long before the term became fashionable. She grew up in an era when a woman's place was in the home and told a *Register* reporter in 1980: "My husband was always against my working. I had to be there for the children, keep the house clean, and have supper on the table, if I wanted to work." Life wasn't easy. It could also be frustrating. Regarding her earlier unsuccessful bids for city council she said in that same interview, "There are women who won't vote for women, and a lot of women who would like to get involved but don't because their husbands won't let them, or they just don't have the time."

Today Delia Donne lives at Stillwater Pond next door to her daughter. It's a well maintained condo filled with shelves of family photos (to include 3 grandchildren). Dee is fashionably thin and sharply dressed. Her voice is still that raspy, deep one people associate with her. Her mind is quick, her eyes alert. Above the fireplace hangs a large family portrait (right). It's a reminder that for Delia, life was, and always will be, family first. That caring and love take center stage.

That she fit Torrington into the mix for a long, extended period, we're blessed and grateful for. And are damn happy about it.

Sky-Vue Drive-In Theatre
"Top Of The Hill"

(August 29, 2016. After completing the Delia Donne article, I took a long break from writing to rest, to resume work on home maintenance projects, and also to improve the photo quality in my first 2 Torrington books. I also had to master a new computer and a newer version of Photoshop. Once those distractions were over, there was never any doubt in my mind what the next article would be. . . For many of us, the Sky-Vue Drive-In Theatre on Torringford West Street was an important part of growing up. NOTE: There are various spellings and punctuations for that drive-in theater. But, I have used the one here that the Torrington Sky-Vue management used in the earliest *Register* ads. . . And now as the sun sets and night begins to fall, let us settle back, turn up the speaker, and roll the feature.)

They started in the 1930s but didn't hit their height of popularity until the 1950s and '60s. During those 2 decades there were often more people sitting in their cars watching movies than there were sitting indoors at old time conventional theaters.

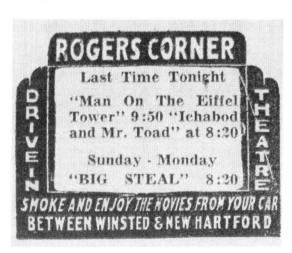

Drive-in theaters in this country were a post-WWII phenomenon that defined summer enter-tainment for many. In this area the first drive-in was built in Bark-hamsted by the Youmatz family around 1947. It went by 2 names: the Rogers Corner Drive-In and also the Pleasant Valley Drive-In (Above, a 1949 ad). In the late 1940s there was also an drive-in on Route 7 in Canaan.

The first drive-in in Torrington was the aptly named Torrington Drive-In, and it opened in August 1950. It was located in Burrville on the Winsted Road just north of Burr Mountain Road on the left. And while popular from the first, it took second stage for many once the Sky-Vue Drive-In Theatre opened on Wednesday, May 9, 1951 (Right, the original ad). The 10-acre tract of land on Torring-ford West had been sold by Dick's owner Richard T. Cooke to Vincent You-matz in April of 1950.

Vin Youmatz, the son: "My father built it and my family ran it until 1963. That new steel screen, the largest in the northeast at the time, was built in 1958 after the wooden one was blown down by a major storm/hurricane(?) that summer. I used to spend my summers cleaning up trash and fixing speakers in the morning and being a gofer at night before settling in to watch the movies. Great times. My best memory was climbing the back of the screen when I was a young teen to try to change the lights at the top (not sure I ever quite made it all the way up)."

When the Sky-Vue opened in 1951, it was competing with indoor movies at the Warner (*Hamlet* with Laurence Olivier), the State, and the Palace (*I Can Get It For You Wholesale* with Susan Hayward).

But there was something about that new outdoor theater that attracted local people immediately. It was a good deal, e.g. 50¢ per adult admission and children under 12 free. For that price patrons got 2 feature movies, 3 cartoons, and a newsreel. A great deal, and while other indoor *and* outdoor theaters offered similar prices and playbills, no one could match the modern rest rooms, a baby nursery where bottles could be warmed, and a new children's playground. . . No doubt Sky-Vue's newness played into its immediate success, i.e. who doesn't like the most up-to-date. . . There was also the issue of bugs/mosquitoes, and the general feeling that the Burrville theater was home to more of the flying insects because of the proximity of the woods and wetlands. The Sky-Vue being at "the top of the hill" at least *seemed* more bug-free. . . But perhaps the major thing Sky-Vue had over the other theaters, certainly over the other drive-ins, was its central location. What could be an easier destination for locals than a venue sandwiched between East Main and the New Harwinton Road?

The Sky-Vue was here to stay.

And the neighborhood kids loved it.

Rich Arnista: "The Sky-Vue was 50 yards away from my backyard. I could hear and watch the movie while playing hoops in my yard. The worst part was when we were sleeping and something went wrong with the film; all the cars beeping woke us up. . . There were many kids who went through our yard so they didn't have to pay. They'd get inside, then jump into their friend's car. My dad finally put a fence up, though maybe we should have charged them a cheaper price and made some money on it! . . . We called those rocks out back where the kids would sit after they snuck in, the 'stage coach rocks.' There were three rocks each smaller than the other. . . One year the Sky-Vue was kept opened in winter. That was not a good decision. . . I'll always remember when the wind knocked the screen over. Just minutes before it happened, my sis and I were walking to Torringford School. Our Mom was frantic thinking we were under the rubble."

(Left, a yardstick from the Sky-Vue and Torrington Drive-Ins which states, "Movies Are Great In 68")

Lucille Fines: "I lived on Torringford West Street 3

96

houses down from the Sky-Vue. We moved there on January 21, 1956, which was my second birthday. Back then it was all woods all the way to East Main. . . I have wonderful memories of the Sky-Vue. During the day my friends and I would sneak in and turn up the speakers in the last row. Then at night we'd sneak back through the woods from Stars with our flashlights and pieces of cardboard to sit on. That's how we'd watch the movies. There were the Tofields, the Beyers, and us, the Schallers."

Looking to beat the price of admission was commonplace, and many former kids, tweens, and teens remember doing just that at the Sky-Vue.

Shawn Martinez: "We used to watch movies for free out back. We'd sit on the rocks and watch 'em."

Judy Michael: "I grew up on Scott Drive and also used to sit on the rocks to watch the shows."

Rose Marie Romanelli: "Wow, I remember the Sky-Vue Drive-In. I was a regular with family and friends. I can remember trying to jam as many people into the car as possible."

Gordon Richard: "Some buddies and I used to crawl under the fern trees that bordered Stars and the Sky-Vue and watch from there!"

Jon McKeone: "The last time I saw a film at the Sky-Vue, we snuck in from the Stars' lot and sat by a speaker in the back to watch *Up In Smoke*." (1978)

Tom Piccolo: "I remember being with my friend Paul and putting Eileen and Lissa in the trunk of my father's Olds. We did it in the Stars' parking lot. (Below, teens caught stuffing a trunk.) I can't

believe they let us talk them into it. Then we snuck them in. The girls thought it was funny. I don't remember the movie."

Charlene O'Neil: "I remember packing in friends in the trunk and going. Thankfully, nobody suffocated!"

Karen Parente Beauchemin: "I remember one time taking my sister to the Sky-Vue, and the gate attendant saying to to us, 'I won't charge you for the 6 kids in the trunk.' Seems that people did that."

Nancy Reynolds: "I remember sneaking through the woods in the dark and hoping you could find the right car."

Linda Torson Volpi: " I hid in the trunk with friends to get into the Sky-Vue for free. What wasn't funny was when we drove to the Watertown Drive-In, and some of us were in the trunk. They just drove around while we were suffocating and banging on the trunk hood!"

(Above, the Sky-Vue in 1974 with the Goodyear Blimp overhead. The blimp was over Torrington to celebrate Toce Brothers 50th anniversary. Photo credit to Rich Arnista.)

Not all young people snuck in. Many of the *very* young were brought to the Sky-Vue by their parents so the movie could act as a type of surrogate babysitter, i.e. keep the toddlers entertained.

Chris Pond: "I don't know why I remember this, but my mother and her best friend across the street brought me with them to the Sky-Vue, which was my first time ever there. I absolutely hated it. The movie was *The Nun's Story*, and I was dying in the backseat the whole time. I must have been too young to be left behind. However, I would have been fine with my toy soldiers. Some years later, my memories became much more pleasant in the '63 Plymouth."

Linda L. Baldwin: "I remember bringing my son to see the first *Star Wars* movie at the Sky-Vue. Good memories."

Karen Parente Beauchemin: "When we were little, I remember playing on the swings at the Sky-Vue and eating popcorn."

At the Sky-Vue there was a playground of sorts down by the screen where youngsters entertained themselves till dusk and the start of the night's cinematic showings. I remember myself going to the Sky-Vue as a small fry in my PJs and falling asleep in the backseat while my parents sat up front, smoked, and enjoyed the feature.

For most teens even today, turning 16 means getting a driver's license. And back in the drive-in era that had special meaning.

Bill Ryan: There was this dividing line. Were you 16 *before* the summer of your rising Junior Year? *Or* were you 15? I was the latter, so, I could not drive to the Sky-Vue until the NEXT summer (so far away, like the next century). But, if you had a classmate who *did* have his/her driver's license (and permission to use the family car), you could go as a passenger in the back seat on a double date. Which I did in 1966, and which I will never forget."

(Above, Sandy and Danny at the drive-in movie just before he makes his big "move," and she bolts. I believe Torrington male teens had better luck.)

Carol Guerrini Gergley: "I remember double dating at the drive-in with my twin sister in the 1960s."

Nancy Reynolds: "Saturday night was date night at the Sky-Vue. All those fogged up windows."

Hartley "Bud" Connell (long time projectionist at the Sky-Vue): "Romance? At the drive-in? My memory is as foggy regarding that as were the car windows of my father's 1963 Ford Galaxy. . . I also worked one summer as manager of the Torrington Drive-In, and there was one time when I thought I had 2 dead people. The car was parked way up in the back. It was still there after everyone left. I walked over and at first didn't see anyone. Then I did. Two guys, one with his arm around the other. Luckily it wasn't carbon monoxide poisoning. . ."

The drive-in in general, and the Sky-Vue in particular, meant for local teens a safe haven for "forbidden" things like love, romance, sex, smoking, and booze.

My own most memorable experience involved my first date with my future wife, Karen Perzanowski, in the summer of 1965. She was a girl I'd had my eye on for some time, but the stars had never been in the proper alignment until that '65 night under the darkened heavens on Torringford West. I don't remember the movies, do most teens? We were in my family's Olds F-85. which like most cars back then, had regular straight seats, sort of like a couch, i.e. definitely not the separation of bucket seats. For the first movie she was over by the passenger door. Logistics mean a lot, and this was a seemingly unbreachable gulf. When I came back from the concession stand, she was in front of the radio, i.e. very close. Apparently she had slid over while I was waiting for popcorn. She denies it to this day, but, no matter. Physical closeness + teens = makeout session. Six years later we were married. After Thought: Had F-85s back then been equipped with bucket seats, who knows what would or would *not* have happened. . .

Linda Torson Volpi: "I saw *Goldfinger* with Jim Hoffman in his Chevy Impala convertible through foggy windows. We took vodka, etc., from our parents' supply, in baby food jars; bought orange juice from the snack bar; and made screwdrivers to watch the movies with."

Doris Russo Richards: "Hmmm. I remember Jack (Richards, future husband) and I went to the same movie for 3 nights and never did finish it. The good old days. They were the best."

Sandy Richard: "The difference between going to the indoor and outdoor theaters was that you never cared about what was playing at the outdoor."

Perhaps Donna McGrane, the current owner of the Pleasant Valley Drive-In, summed up the sex angle best in a recent magazine article when she said: "I have older people who pull in and say, 'Our first child was conceived here!' "

Sex. Drive-in sex. It was very popular. As was booze.

Hartley "Bud" Connell: "It was BYOB, and there was no shortage of coolers or empty Bud cans at the Sky-Vue. I can't remember if Connecticut paid for returnables back in those 1970's days, but the grounds were a mess after a busy night, for sure. Critters had a feast after the cars left. Thankfully, no bears were around as they are now!"

No one ever raved about Sky-Vue food, woodland critters aside. I seldom had enough money to buy anything but popcorn, if that. Food was an afterthought, at least to me. Not so for everyone. I once took a date to the Sky-Vue who didn't look like a big eater. But when intermission rolled around and I asked her if she wanted anything, she said, "I'll have a Coke, a hot dog, popcorn, and pizza." I nearly passed out. She wasn't kidding, and I finally had to confess that I only had enough money for *one* item. We never dated again.

(Above, the Sky-Vue concession stand, the bermed earth, and the back of Stars. Photo credit Rich Arnista.)

Sandy Richard: "I didn't care for the Sky-Vue food. We'd stop at Tony's before and get Rich Man Grinders (ham, salami, capicola, cheese, peppers, lettuce, tomatoes, and sauce for $1.25). . . Most girls on a date would order just a soda."

Alanne Kennedy Turina: "Charlie and I tended to skip the food at the Sky-Vue. We'd stop at McDonald's (fairly new at the time) after the movies for a burger, fries, and shake."

John Todor: "Gotta love the dancing conga line of popcorn, hot dogs, and hamburgers at intermission. 'The show will resume in five minutes.' Was it just me, or did that 15 minute intermission seem to last for two hours?. . . Of course I ate the popcorn, but the hot dogs weren't bad either. You really have to go some to mess up a hot dog."

Mary Lee and Will Point: "Both our kids puked all over the car. So much for Sky-Vue food. That was in the early 1960s. It was our last family drive-in visit."

Nancy Reynolds: "For some reason I remember the ice cream cones. They were filled to the top of the cone. That's all, but the whole cone was filled with ice cream. It was flat on the top. It sounds crazy, but I really liked the chocolate. Those were some good times."

Hartley "Bud" Connell: "Aside from popcorn, soda, and packaged (wrapped) candy, I wouldn't touch the food. Example - hamburgers were kept in a crock pot in a barbecue sauce. Didn't sell? No problem. Just reheat and sell the next evening! Rolls were never thrown out, just softened up in a steam warmer until you opened a new package and started the same process over again. . . Burgers, which were frozen raw, were put into bubbling sauce where they 'cooked.' Hot dogs were cooked in slow rotisserie, and arrived in bulk from a food distributor, as did most of the food such as #10 cans of meatballs. Gross things that were prepared as hamburgers. Pizzas came with frozen crusts. Then you added heated sauce and mozzarella, put them in a counter pizza oven/warmer, and served 'piping hot' as the intermission film between shows would proclaim. Understand that the concession people made due with what equipment they had working, so there were many variations from all this."

Of course the Sky-Vue, as any and all theaters, was supposed to be primarily about the movies themselves. And in its heyday of the 1950s and '60s, the Sky-Vue *did* get the popular, first run films. Examples: Back in May 1965 "Marriage Italian Style" with Sophia Loren, "Ride The Wild Surf" with Fabian and Shelley Fabares, "Love With The Proper Stranger" with Steve McQueen and Natalie

Wood, and "Splendor In the Grass" were paired in the same week. Movies pairings generally showed Wednesday–Saturday, with new movies starting Sunday and running through Tuesday. Lesser quality films, such as "The Horror Of Party Beach" and "The Curse Of The Living Corpse," might play for one Sunday night only, as those did in 1965. . . Gates opened at 7:30; the first feature was at dusk. The Sky-Vue itself had a 575 car capacity, and a neon marquee heralded the night's showings. The old Sky-Vue wooden screen had internal storage for the marquee letters, according to Vin Youmatz.

When the Torrington Drive-In first began, according to one old time veteran, there were only 2 speakers: large ones on the screen itself. This led to the humorous image of a lot full of cars, windows rolled down, heads sticking out to hear the soundtrack.

Individual speakers for each car at the Sky-Vue hung on metal posts. You would pull alongside, and hook a speaker onto your partially rolled down window. (Below, an original Sky-Vue speaker.)

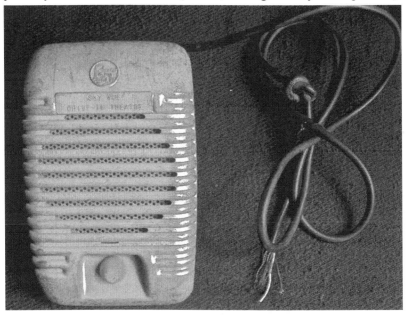

Lovers might turn the volume off, or not even put put the speaker in the car. Those who did, always ran the risk of forgetting to put it back on the post as they zoomed off trying to beat the other 500+ cars to the exit. John Todor: "Who can forget the sound of breaking glass as someone drove off without first taking the speaker off the window."

Vin Youmatz: "On morning cleanup I'd find car parts (bumpers, etc.) left behind, along with the downed speaker posts and ripped out speakers."

The audio portion of the movie was improved with individual car speakers. And the visual image was improved with a new metal screen in 1958, which was HUGE! by comparison. The physical layout of the Sky-Vue's 11.66 acres was also conducive to pleasurable viewing. The screen tilted forward to help enable cars a clearer view, even those in the last row 400 feet away. The earth was bermed in rows, and the rows themselves were slightly concave as they flexed around the screen. The berms elevated the cars (front grills pointing towards the sky like hound dogs baying at the moon) for an unobstructed view. And the concession stand was constructed low for the same purpose. Ted Dunn: "It was fun riding a bicycle fast from the back of the Sky-Vue down to the screen over all those humps between lanes (rows)."

It was important with quality movies to have qualified, certified projectionists who knew what they were doing. Hartley "Bud" Connell was just that man from 1973-'80.

Hartley Connell: "I enjoyed being the projectionist. Working with my hands around machines in an isolated environment was so different from teaching (Connell taught for decades at Vogel-Wetmore and the Torrington Middle School). Nice change of pace that fit my teaching schedule. We had two machines of the carbon-arc variety. Each reel was 17 to 20 minutes long, then you changed over to the next reel. Cues were white dots in top right corner of screen. First set of dots told you to start the second machine (bring it up to speed). When the second set of dots flashed, you had to begin projecting the other reel and shutting down the first machine. You then rewound that reel of film and put new reel on to start the same process all over again. I mostly corrected papers or read in the booth, which was soundproof. Some films I watched repeatedly because I enjoyed them. It just depended. . ."

Connell had been a manager at the Torrington Drive-In before becoming the projectionist at the Sky-Vue. Why the change? "The money was better being a projectionist. I made $50 for showing 2 films. I had to join the union and was president at one point." Not only was the money better, but Connell confessed that occasionally the hours could be better, i.e. cut shorter. . . "One season I worked with Newell Porch as the manager. If Newell needed to leave early, he would come into the booth and suggest editing the film. That meant I would cut away from one reel early and start the next machine (reel) late. By the end of the two shows we could knock off half-an-hour. Only got caught once in a Brooke Shields film called *The Blue Lagoon*. A customer who had seen the film in a regular theater went to Newell and complained. Newell brought the fellow into the booth, and we both expressed shock, then outrage that the distributor would send us a faulty print!"

When not being cut short, the quality of films for over 2 decades was superb. Vin Youmatz: "I had to shuttle canisters of film reels between the Sky Vue and the Warner when a first run picture was being shown at both places and there were not enough prints available at the distributor."

That is not to say that B-pictures, horror, monster, sexploitation, etc. were never shown. Usually, before school got out for the summer, the cheaper rentals got played. Sometimes only for one night, and usually on a slow night like Sunday. But as the 1960s turned into the '70s, slowly over that time frame the quality deteriorated. By this time the Youmatz family had sold out. On March 5, 1965, Henry G. Youmatz sold the Sky-Vue to Torringford Amusement Corporation, Inc. (President Arthur Lockwood) for an undisclosed sum but with a $60,000 down payment. In August 1969 The Torringford Amusement Corporation sold the Sky-Vue to Sonderling Broadcasting Corp. of New York for $220,000.

Though the Sky-Vue had always had plenty of competition, it seemed to intensify as time passed. During the latter part of the 1960s the main local competition came from Wright's, the Sugar Shack (with "Linda," the Sugar Shack Dancer), the Music Box, Teddy's A Go Go, The Place (often featuring Tom Coury and The Party Cats), et al. By 1974, Mondays and Tuesdays at the Sky-Vue were often 99¢/person, and who wouldn't like and use a free

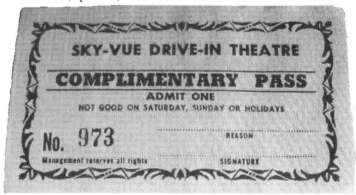

Complimentary Pass (the profit was in the concession stand anyway). In the meanwhile the SBC Management Corporation, which owned *both* the Sky-Vue and the Torrington Drive-In, was starting to come under fire for showing "revealing" movies. Complaints were received by town officials that passersby on the highway alongside the Torrington Drive-In could see "boobs." There was also a one-man campaign in 1974 by Rev. James Dollar of the Church Of Christ who wanted a city ordinance passed after he said he observed "several dozen children and young persons watching the X-rated *Teach Me* at the Sky-Vue."

The SBC Management Corporation, which owned both Torrington drive-ins, pledged in July 1974 *not* to show any X-rated movies pending the outcome of a feasibility study for erecting "sight shields to prevent the viewing from beyond the theaters' premises."

No one I contacted could remember anything ever coming of it.

By the summer of 1980 the Sky-Vue had slipped into showing antique kiddie movies such as *Mary Poppins* and *Sleeping Beauty*. And offering admission for $6 a carload. Movies were kept longer, and there were fewer "new" movies. The days of operation were cut back.

In June 1982, the Planning and Zoning Commission in Torrington received a proposal from Harold Burns and others for a 79-unit elderly housing project. PZC Chairman Nicholas Horansky, who resided in the Sky-Vue area, told the press that the project would be a great improvement to the neighborhood. He said that the theater "has been a thorn in everybody's side up there." And he cited the noise of the movie speakers and the lights. The housing project itself was to be a quality, $4 million expenditure. It had a *lot* of support.

Even as plans to sell it ($300,000 for the land alone) moved forward, the Sky-Vue continued to operate. In June the drive-in showed *The Happy Hooker* ("a real women tells the truth") with Xaviera Hollander and *Private Lessons* ("What happened to him should happen to *you!*"). So much for SBC's 1974 pledge against X-rated cinema. Meanwhile, in the North End across from K-Mart, the Holiday 6 Cinema was featuring the current blockbusters *Star Trek II, Rocky III, Conan The Barbarian, Dead Men Don't Wear Plaid*, et al. And this indoor multiplex was raking it in.

In late June 1982 the housing project was approved, and on October 6, 1982, ground was broken on Torringford West Street.

The nights of the Sky-Vue Drive-In were over. It was soon physically gone.

What killed the Sky-Vue? An easy answer would be *time*. Time brought in rising gas prices, multiplexes with comfortable seats and A/C, cable tv, VCRs and video rentals, distant corporate ownership, and a changing local economy.

In fact, the death knell came from many directions.

But though gone, the Sky-Vue has not been forgotten by those who frequented the "Top Of The Hill" amphitheatre. Sandra Lucia Calkins and Miles Concannon both had parents who worked there and both remembered spending much of their youth at the Sky-Vue, Calkins "cleaning up the drive-in and making popcorn."

Sandy Richard: "The Sky-Vue was *the* thing to do in the summer. It was *the* place to be with friends. Or a new date. You could talk. Get to know each other. . . We had it *all*."

On those soft summer nights of so long ago, we indeed just *might* have had it all. . .

(Above, dusk sets on a bygone era. The chirping of crickets and the awakening of nightbirds. The flaring hemline of an early evening sky heralding showtime, and a world and life we thought would last forever.)

Dick's Restaurant
A Legendary Torrington Oasis

(September 10, 2016. When writing about Torrington places, I like to choose spots that are well known and that for many furnish a common experience. As far as Torrington restaurants go, there never has been, and just might never be again, a watering hole with the stature of Dick's. Special thanks to Gale Yurgalevicz Colangelo who, in her efforts to move on, was willing to step back and provide many pictures and much information concerning the years the Colangelos owned Dick's. Also thanks to Eddie Janssen for allowing me access to the "official" Dick's sports scrapbook that his brother Charlie compiled, and to a myriad of Ed's own memories. To the many others who contributed their reminiscences including Pat Colangelo, Billy's widow. Finally to Richard T. Cooke and brothers Vito "Billy" and Raymond "Brooklyn" Colangelo – a trio of fine restaurateurs whose vision, hard work, and congeniality made Dick's the #1 dining and drinking spot in Torrington for over 60 years.)

The outside of 26 East Main featured hunter green awnings on 2 levels, horizontal slit windows, a polished gray stone exterior, and a suspended dark green sign with gold carved lettering proudly proclaiming "Dick's Restaurant." The lettering was highlighted by simple gold scrollwork within a golden painted border. In earlier decades, the 1955 Flood years for example, there had been plainer lettering affixed to the building itself: D I C K' S (slight lean to the right on the "S").

Entering by the front door, which was on the right as you faced the restaurant, you came into a small vestibule. There were stairs straight ahead leading upstairs to "Louis The Tailor" where Louis O. Farrace worked his craft. After he retired, that space became Dick's banquet hall. (Below, the original metal sign, with "shadowed" black and red lettering on a yellow background.)

But most took the inside door to the left which brought you into a milk chocolate, wood-paneled hall lined with awards and plaques containing, for example, the names of scholarship winners. Down the hall was the 2-tier dining room where on a Saturday night diners crowded the tables, perhaps trying to squeeze in a meal before a Warner show. Straight ahead from the vestibule was the bar with classy real-wood paneling and wine-red brick walls. Those walls held a mosaic of sports memorabilia, many inscribed to "Brooklyn," and most a tribute to Notre Dame football and NY Yankee baseball. A tv would be on in the upper right corner behind the bar and most likely would be tuned to a game or ESPN. There would be a sense as in the fictional bar "Cheers" that this was a place where everyone knew your name. Or if not, would take you quickly into the conversation and bonhomie that pervaded the high-ceiling room.

Dick's. The unofficial sports headquarters of Torrington. It was a restaurant, a bar. The gathering spot where for the price of a drink or a meal you could forget your troubles and become part of something larger. An unofficial club/fraternal organization. And it had started a very long time ago. . .

For nearly over a century there had been a restaurant in that lower East Main block. The previous restaurant (18 East Main) had not been *quite* where Dick's would be (26 East Main). Back in the 1910s and '20s it was owned by John J. Miran whose daughter Esther (THS '34) would marry Seymour Franklin. Both would become Torrington teachers. John Miran sold it to William F. Sonnenburg in 1926, and in September 1941 Sonnenburg, through the Edward J. Burns Realty company, sold it to Richard T. Cooke and Matthew J. Considine. Cooke was the previous proprietor of Central Sea Food while Considine had owned Walcon, a billiard and bowling establishment. The newest owners combined their names and created the "Dick & Matt Restaurant." (Left, a souvenir matchbook from the early 1940s.) It was the first coupling of the name "Dick" with a Torrington restaurant. The restaurant quickly became highly regarded, according to a *Register* article, and served patrons from all over Northwest Connecticut. Each man in the process establishing "an enviable reputation."

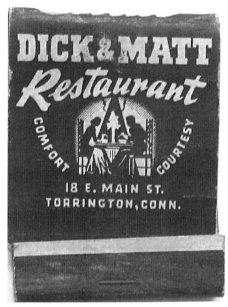

By 1945 Cooke and Considine were ready to strike out on their own. Considine would keep the 18 East Main space and would now team with his brothers James A. and Frank. The new "Considine's" would become larger, expanding into the adjoining store to the west. Cooke would move a couple of store fronts east to 26 East Main. Dick & Matt Restaurant stayed open till both former partners were ready to open their new and separate restaurants. It was felt that the general public and modern Torringtonites depended more than ever on restaurants for meals especially with the food rationing of WWII. The restaurants would be physically close with only Sears separating them. Sort of Torrington's version of NYC's Restaurant Row. But it was a friendly rivalry with more than enough customers to go around. (Below, the aftermath of the 1955 Flood which both restaurants survived.)

Richard T. Cooke, a.k.a. "Dick," decided to go with an eponymous, casual name for his new restaurant and called it simply "Dick's." It opened on October 30, 1945, not quite 2 months after VJ-Day and WWII. (Right, the original *Register* ad).

Richard "Dick" Cooke was a popular man whose personable ways were a good fit for a victualler. He was in numerous fraternal and religious clubs/organizations, was a founder and president of the Elks Glee Club, head of the Rod & Gun Club, member of Torrington's Safety Board, and a candidate for Democratic State Senator in 1954 (defeated). During a February 1950 testimonial

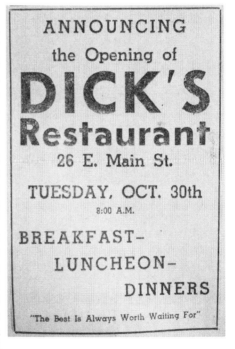

ANNOUNCING

the Opening of

DICK'S

Restaurant

26 E. Main St.

TUESDAY, OCT. 30th
8:00 A.M.

BREAKFAST–

LUNCHEON–

DINNERS

"The Best Is Always Worth Waiting For"

dinner in his honor when he was appointed to a 6-year term on the state Fish and Game Commission, Connecticut's Lt. Governor William Carroll was among the many speakers and 200 guests. Carroll paid tribute to Cooke as a "sportsman and outstanding citizen." Speeches were given by such people as William O'Donnell, sports editor of *The Waterbury Republican*, Senator Samuel Blakeslee, and Dr. Russell Hunter, superintendent of the state board of fisheries and game.

The *nephew* of Dick Cooke (the restaurant founder in picture on left), himself named "Dick Cooke" (THS 1966), recently said of his late uncle: "He was a good guy. Good to everyone. And generous. When he and Mattie (Considine) broke up, he'd lend him things like bottles of liquor. Regulars like Jack Tucker and Huddie Thayer told me in later years, 'Your uncle really knew how to run a bar and restaurant.' "

The younger Cooke remembered that as a youngster back in the 1950s he and his family would go to Dick's Restaurant every Sunday after church for a big family meal. "No one in my family ever paid for anything," the nephew recalled. "I'd be thirsty and walking past, and just go in and get something to drink. My uncle sponsored a professional baseball team that he made no money on. He just loved baseball."

It's an old adage in the restaurant business that being generous comes back many times over. Dick Cooke, the restaurateur, gave of his money and in doing so multiplied his own. Having money to invest now, he became a savvy wheeler-dealer. According to his nephew, "Uncle Dick bought up a lot of land on upper East Main." This he sold in part to Vincent Youmatz (p.95) for the Sky-Vue Drive-In, and sold more in part to the Temkins for residential housing. A blessed man who was reaping the good he sowed.

It didn't last.

Richard T. Cooke died in February 1956. He was only 53-years-old. The restaurant, newly renovated and refurbished after the August

'55 Flood, had reopened only a few weeks earlier. Did the physical and mental strain of trying to rebound do Richard T. Cooke in? Did, in fact, saving and bringing his restaurant back from the abyss kill him? We'll never know. . . For the next decade his brother John ("Jake"), and after him Jake's son Paul, who had gone to culinary school, tried to keep Dick's Restaurant going under the auspices of Dick's widow Mae (née Richard). But according to young Dick, it never really took off, or even stayed the same. Something wasn't clicking. Sidebar: Restaurants and their patrons are held together by a fragile mix, tenuous bonds. When it's right, business can boom. When it isn't, . . .

By 1966 the business at 26 Main Street was listed as "vacant."

❖ ❖ ❖ ❖

While Dick's Restaurant was struggling to survive following the death of its founder, 2 Italian brothers were rising stars in their own right. Vito "Billy" and Raymond "Brooklyn" Colangelo were brothers who shared more than just an uterine relationship. Both were born and raised in Torrington. Both loved baseball. Both had co-cap-

tained their THS nines: Billy in 1953, Brook in 1958. Both were Army veterans; Billy served in Korea, Brook in Alaska. And both worked in The Tor-rington Company following their discharges. (Above, a Torrington Co. softball team circa late 1950s. Billy Colangelo is in a dark shirt in the front row).

Around 1961, Billy broke out of the factory and partnered with Frank Eucalitto. Together they started Frank & Bill's Tavern at 156

East Main (around where Vinny's Restaurant & Pizzeria is today). Two years later in 1963, they moved closer to the center of town when they rented the old Coachman Restaurant with the Hotel Lawrence above. The partners opened Colitto's Restaurant there at 46 East Main, only a few doors up from Dick's. The name was a combination of "Colangelo" and "Eucalitto." At some point in the early 1960s, Brooklyn quit the factory and joined his brother in Colitto's. (Below, Brooklyn on left and Billy on right posing in Colitto's bar between 1963 and 1967.)

Eddie Janssen: "I started hanging around with the Colangelos in 1955 after the Flood. I spent more time with them than I did at home. Spent a lot of time with Andy."

The 2 Colangelo brothers had a lot of friends like Eddie Janssen and other sports-minded people. But they also knew many others and had established a base of loyal customers in mastering the restaurant and bar business. By late fall 1967, after Dick's had been listed as "vacant" for 2 years, the Cooke and Colangelo families were ready for something to happen. Something that would transform Dick's for the next 51 years.

Dick Cooke (nephew): "A lot of people wanted to take over Dick's. But my Aunt Mae was very fussy. She really liked 'both of those boys' (Vito/Billy and Raymond/Brook), as she called them. They had to promise *not* to change the name."

114

On December 1, 1967, Dick's Restaurant got an infusion of new blood. And a new lease on life. It reopened with the Colangelo brothers as the new owners.

(Above, December 1, 1967, the grand opening. A ribbon cutting ceremony in the upper tier of the dining room. L-R: City Clerk Fred Bruni, Martin Harris from Brooks Bank, Billy Colangelo, Yolanda Colangelo, Mayor P. Edmund Power, Attorney Joe Gallicchio, Brook Colangelo, father Joseph "Pike" Colangelo, designer Armand DeAngelis, mother Lucy Colangelo, and Francis Hennessy from Hartford National Bank.)

Pat Colangelo (Billy's wife and head waitress at Dick's for 42 years, starting 2 weeks after they opened): "Louie the tailor always claimed it was his idea that Billy and Brook buy Dick's. He claimed he told them (when they ran Colitto's), 'Why don't you buy the place over there (Dick's)?' Years later when they were trying to raise his rent, Louie flat out refused. Said, 'You wouldn't even *have* the place if it wasn't for me.' He was old school. A big laugh. No one was upset. Louie was a good egg. They never *did* raise his rent."

According to Pat Colangelo, once the Colangelo brothers took over, Dick's was pretty much a success from the beginning. She recalled, "Thursday night when downtown was open, store workers who had to go back to work started coming in at 4:30. The bar was 3-deep. People couldn't get in. Thursday-to-Saturday was really big;

you needed reservations. We had many regulars like Bernie Rubino who never missed a New Year's party, Jack Tucker, the Chadwick family, Dee when she was mayor, Owen Quinn, Mike Conway and Mike Merati. A lot of 'characters' too. Quirky. Kicker Fabbri's father was so huge he needed both doors open to come in." Gail Colangelo added the names Harry Purcell and Huddy Thayer as early regulars.

During those early years Gail Colangelo remembered Brook's mother coming in once a week to make the sauce. Eddie Janssen: "I'd see her making the sauce in 2 big kettles at home. Brook would jar it and bring it to the restaurant. She also made the best raviolis."

In those earliest years Billy and Brooklyn both were in the bar. Ray Green ran the kitchen; later his son Joe was head chef for 35 years right up to the time they closed. Joe had the reputation of being excellent in the kitchen and an outstanding grill man. Dick's was the only restaurant in Torrington with an outdoor grill that was in service year-round. Those charcoal grilled steaks, in what was considered an Italian-American restaurant, soon became a signature piece on the bill of fare.

Diane Marie Finello Thompson: "The steak was so good."
Mark Purcell: "I remember the steaks cooked outside."
TJ Jacquot: "The steaks from the outdoor grill were fabulous!!!"
Pat Fairchild: "I enjoyed many meals there, especially the Cajun steak and Irish salad dressing."
Linda Torson Volpi: "I only remember that my mother (or was it my father?) loved the giant stuffed pork chops."
Eddie Janssen: "Billy knew how to cook steaks. The grill in the back must have been grandfathered. Today health officials would shut you down."
John Todor: "I used to eat there a lot. The food was always good, as was the service. I loved to have a steak or chops that they cooked on the outside grill."

Though a lot goes into making a successful restaurant, certainly food is *key*. And while the charcoal grilled steaks and pork chops were immensely popular, favorites were as varied as the diners themselves. Gail Colangelo remembered the baked stuffed shrimp being the best in town. She added how Rico Soliani would bring in homemade sausage and wine and somehow the wine would wind up in the sauce. Nancy Reynolds remembered going to Dick's after church with her parents, and said, "It was a Sunday ritual, and the only time I had a coke and toast for breakfast." My wife, Karen Bentley, favored the veal saltimbocca. Sidebar: Many thought Dick's had the best veal in town, and it would be difficult to argue otherwise. For an appetizer I personally favored the sausage and spinach sauteed with garlic.

Chris Pond: "Best pomodoro sauce, period. Brooklyn gave me the recipe along with how he made his antipasto. It's kind of like when a grandparent passes and you realize you are never going to taste a certain food ever again. . . The braciole was also out of this world."

Shelley Considine: "Dick's was always the go-to place for a good meal. . . It was THE go-to place when I was pregnant. With our first, I craved grilled cheeseburgers, steak fries, and coleslaw. Had to be the complete craving, so off to Dick's it was. Needless to say I always got my complete order. During my second pregnancy, the craving was bagels, so no Dick's connection there. But for the third it was Dick's steak salad with curly fries on top and Irish dressing. . . They only served it for lunch, unless they saw me waddling in at dinner. It was the best."

(Below, undated photo of Monica and Jimmy Doyle dining at Dick's bar)

A very popular food at Dick's was pizza, which, unfortunately, if a person didn't like watching football, he/she probably never ate at 26 East Main.

Pat Colangelo: "The pizza making tradition started on Sunday. Billy said, 'For the heck of it, why don't you make a pizza?' It started with one pizza for the guys watching the game."

Chris Pond: "Brooklyn had the best pizza in town. What most people did not realize, it was only served during halftime during

Monday night football. They were all speciality pies, like keilbasa, spinach, and countless others. They were served at the bar piece-by-piece, depending on your pleasure. You would put $10 in the bucket when you came in, and the drinks were included. Bob Bastasini was somehow in charge of all this, or at least the tip for the pizza makers."

Once the pizza and Monday Night Football were a firmly established tradition at Dick's, the pizzas, according to Pat Colangelo, were made by herself, Nancy Hogan, and Marie Recidivi. I only stopped in one time on a Monday night, and I don't remember the drinks being included for a flat rate. But I do remember dropping a sum of money in the tip jar and Brooklyn telling me it was "too much." Naturally he wanted to do right by the hard working ladies making the pizzas. *But*, he also wanted to keep expenses down for his patrons, especially the regulars, and probably did not want me upsetting the balance.

The Regulars: Over the decades the faces changed as one generation replaced another. I was *not* a regular, though I stopped in the

bar occasionally on a Friday night, and my wife and I ate occasionally in the dining room on Saturday. The people I remember the most are Holly and Biff Pond, Chris Pond, (Professor) Gershom Foster, Jimmy Doyle, Mark "Ziff" Riechenberg, Bernie Rubino, John Brennan, RJ Poniatoski, Mickey Bonasera, Rick Myers, Tommy McLaughlin, Jay and Pam Cilfone, Adele and Rit Zaharek, et al. The bartender was Bruce Kovalaski; Angelo Bonasera before him. When the kitchen closed on Sundays, Brooklyn would make food for the bar regulars and he'd put out grinders, pasta, meatballs, and by 1 p.m. the bar would be packed. No charge for the food.

(Picture above, Bernie Rubino in his favorite seat under the tv and by the swinging, dining room doors with Gail Colangelo next to him.)

The bar regulars were predominantly men, and predominately men who like watching and talking about sports. Pat Colangelo: "All our customers were very close. Very few who didn't fit in, sports wise. People had the same bar seats. Came in at the same time. Left the same tip. There would be a big hullabaloo if someone was in someone else's seat/table."

There was a strong sense of comradery. Many of the regulars drank together, ate together, and sometimes went to games together. Brooklyn had a nucleus of fellows who traveled to South Bend, Indiana, every year for a Notre Dame football game (right). They went to Final Fours. Attended

each other's weddings. Note: Link Jones got married upstairs in the banquet hall, as did others. Regulars supported the annual Dick's Clam Bake and Scholarship Dinner/Fund.

Gail herself met Brooklyn at Dick's in March 1968. "I was a secretary at Fitzie's (Fitzgerald's) and stopped in for lunch. Brook asked Vinnie Testanero who I was. We talked. The rest is history." Two months later the couple eloped on a Sunday in May. They drove to Baltimore for the ceremony, but not before stopping at Yankee Stadium to watch a game. Gail would go on to become a secretary at City Hall and a full time mother. She would not begin waitressing at Dick's until 1983 when daughter Tina Marie (today a teacher) was 12-years-old and son Brook (today a Chief Information Officer with Houghton Mifflin) was 5. Waitressing allowed her flexible hours and enough time to be a mother and also to be "the rock" of the family. Dick's demanded long hours, 7-days-a-week. And someone had to put the time in. It was Brooklyn and Billy.

Gail Colangelo: " I had a rule that Brooklyn had to be home by 3 a.m. I'd call and say he had to get home. He and the guys would just be sitting around and 'discussing life.' He'd put on Jack Tucker who would say to me, 'Come on, give him another 15 minutes' . . . Brook was a clean-a-holic. We only closed for 10-11 days in the summer. He'd spend the shutdown time cleaning everything including rugs, while I went on vacation by myself. . . He knew the building, every crack. . . He had a passion for taking care of people. We were one big family."

The idea of Dick's "family" goes beyond comradery and sports talk.

Pat Colangelo: "We called them 'mercy dinners.' They were for people who couldn't afford it. Anyone who came to the back door got fed. Or customers who had fallen on hard times. We'd bring the food to the house if we knew about it."

Gail Colangelo: "Brook worked with Prime Time (a non-profit to help those with mental illness). He was a gatherer, a collector of people. On Sundays he'd feed the homeless. People like David and George who rode bicycles. If any of the bar guys complained, Brook would tell them, 'Don't worry. It's *my* food, not yours.' "

Tom Piccolo: "A few days after my father's wake and funeral, I was sitting at the bar alone in Dick's when some totally strange man came up to me and asked if I was Dom's kid. Well, he just went off on how what a great guy my father was. This went on all afternoon with total strangers. I never paid for a drink or felt so proud."

John Todor: "You always found someone to talk to when you stopped at the bar for a drink. My Dad would also stop there often, and when he died, Billy and Brook sent us enough food to feed an army. Great restaurant and great owners."

Pat Fairchild: "Dick's Restaurant will always hold a special place in my heart. It was my father's (Peter Sczucka) favorite watering hole and he idolized both Billy and Brooklyn. As kids, we knew its phone number quite well when we needed to reach our father. It truly was a hometown restaurant where one could socialize with many Torringtonians while being made to feel so welcome by the wonderful wait staff. My family could not thank Brooklyn enough for the kindnesses he showed to us when my father passed away. The Colangelo brothers gave Torrington something that can never be replaced."

Chris Pond: "I used to kid around and say I'm heading down to Dick's 'soup kitchen.' Right up to the day he passed, I used to tell Brooklyn, 'You're the most decent human being I ever met.' And he knew I meant it."

Family helps out family, and while the Colangelo brothers were very, very good to their clientele, occasionally the situation would reverse itself.

Eddie Janssen: "Years ago I was putting up tv antennas. Dick's had at least a 30-footer. It had a motor so it could be turned for more channels. More channels equalled more sports, which equalled more people. Sunday morning of the 'Freezer Bowl' (January 10, 1982) I got a call from Brooklyn. The antenna was down. The morning was freezing cold. By the time we redid the antenna replacing wires and the motor, and getting it all back up, my hands were blue. Billy told me, 'Do you know how much money I would have lost!' "

Family, taking care of family.

Helping to create that sense of "family" was a dedicated and hard working staff to include waitresses Pat and Gail, Lori Ethier, Diane Green, and Angela Grosso – with a lot of people in-between.

(Below, an undated photo of Dick's staff posing in the dining room and looking festive and happy. L-R: Marie Recidivi, Brooklyn, Lori Ethier, Rhonda Ballard, Gail Colangelo, an unknown grill person, Diane Green, Joe Green, Pat Colangelo, Angela Grosso.)

Pat Colangelo: "All the waitresses got along great. We'd argue with Billy and Brook, but it was no big deal. They were good bosses. Honest as the day is long. We waitresses never had to worry about a paycheck. Always paid on time."

Gail Colangelo (regarding working with your spouse, who's also your boss): "We had a bar door between us. Brook believed you do not tell people about your personal business, or even let them know. . . The staff was one big family. If someone was off downstairs, she'd often worked upstairs. We all needed the money. . . There was no dumbwaiter; we were the dumbwaiter."

Being the "dumbwaiter," climbing all those stairs to the banquet hall, all those long hours on their feet, etc. was difficult. But staff members were forever cheerful and outgoing. Never surly. And always helpful and compassionate. I remember one time as my wife and I were leaving the dining hall we came upon my old industrial arts teacher, Russell Anderson. He was sitting alone at a small table next to the hallway. I hadn't seen him in decades and stopped to tell him how much I used to enjoy his classes and currently was enjoying his articles in *The Voice* on stamp/coin collecting. It was a short, one-sided conversation. I talked, he smiled, I smiled. And in the background, over his shoulder, a waitress caught my attention and silently mouthed, "He can't hear a word you're saying!" Helpful for me, compassionate towards Mr. Anderson.

While the name Dick's was synonymous with food and good, friendly service in Torrington, in other quarters it was strongly linked to sports and to sports teams.

In the earliest years, back in the late 1940s, Dick Cooke sponsored a professional baseball team, the Torrington Braves, who played in the Colonial League along with teams from Poughkeepsie, Bridgeport, Kingston, Port Chester, New Brunswick, et al. The roster of the Torrington team included solid players like Jim Argeros, Frank Cardegno, Jack Callahan, Bud Mahon, and Ed Musial.

Dick Cooke (nephew): "I met *Stan* Musial at Dick's when I was very young. He was sitting in a booth. His St. Louis Cardinals were probably playing the Giants, and he came to town to see his brother (Ed) play."

The Colonial League folded in 1950, but Dick's and sports would be bonded together for the next half century. Glenn Gemelli: "My father used to watch boxing at Dick's, and I remember going into the bar with him. That was something for a kid." . . . When the Colangelo brothers first bought the restaurant, and for the next 20 years, Dick's sponsored a bowling league with 6 teams. There was never a basketball team, but for 3 seasons, 1979-'81, there was a men's softball team which played to so-so results (won/loss = 23-21). Though the softball team was scarcely noteworthy, fact is, previously most of the players had been together on the Bake Shop slow-pitch team, and from 1966-1978 compiled a 166-53 record with 4 League Championships. Before that there'd been a fast-pitch softball team that didn't lose a game in 3 years.

Eddie Janssen: "The same guys basically played on all the teams. Originally the flag football team was Connio's (Lopardo). Then we were Colitto's, and finally Dick's."

Dick's Flag Football Team. A dynasty. The gold standard. The team everyone wanted to beat, just like the NY Yankees and The Fighting Irish of Notre Dame, which adorned the walls of Dick's bar.

Eddie Janssen: "If you're into sports, you'll understand that we never had superstars. We were *good* athletes. And we played well together. I never had to call anyone to show up. The schedule was in the newspaper. Ten, fifteen minutes before game time they'd start drifting in. Dick Copertino used to go to Misquamicut every summer, and he'd drive back for the games."

Looking over the 1968-'83 rosters of Dick's flag football players, one is struck by the fact that if these were only *good* players, at least there were *many* of them. Every year. Gridiron speedsters like Joey Spina, Phil Alexander, and Davey Jones. Add to that stalwarts like Andy Colangelo, John Dackow, Tom Kucera, John Copertino, Terry and Beaver Musselman, Hy Ruwet, Eddie Barber, Mark Cuozzo, Pete Sczucka, Mike Samele, Chris Sabia, et al.

(Above, Dick's 1975, 9-0, Flag Football League Champions. L-R, front row: Gene Barbero, John Timm, Chris Germano, Butch Seitz, Dave Tino, Steve Kozlak, Len Lopardo. . . Back Row: Charlie Turina, Biff Pond, Jon Scarmana, Nick Testanero, Vin Testanero, Ed Janssen, Bruce Aube, Tom Petrovits, George Rulli, and Coach Charlie Janssen. Hy Ruwet missing.)

Dick's flag football teams, such as the 1975 team (previous page), were well inured to winning and expected to win. They were league champs 9 out of the 16 seasons they played. Compiled a .846 winning percentage. Completed 6 undefeated seasons. Outscored opponents by an almost 3:1 ratio.

Regarding the 1975 season, I was playing for Jim's Garage along with JoJo Noonan, Jack Litke, Don LaRocco, Bill Baier (Canton), Bill O'Connell, Don Ponak, Rick Fasciano, Steve Bogart, and George Perlotto (who would later play for Dick's). We were good, and we were not intimidated by Dick's. We even jumped into an early lead.

George Perlotto: "I remember the first and last plays very clearly. The 1st play was textbook. We started on the 10, and I called a quarterback draw. I had both split ends in tight and went direct snap. We were the only team that did that. I had the ends run crossing routes and had the flanker back run a flag route. By the time I took my 5 step drop back, the middle was wide open. Like taking candy from a baby. They were upset, and we were rolling."

We stayed ahead too and were up by 4 points with around a minute to go. We had Dick's pinned deep in their own territory. It was 4th-and-long for them. The game seemed in-the-bag; Dick's was going *down*!. . . Unfortunately, there was still time, and, moreover,

they didn't think they were beaten.

Chris Germano faded back and threw down-the-middle to Hy Ruwet. Our own Jack Litke was behind Ruwet and right on him. They went up for the pass together. When Hy caught the ball, Jack (who was 6'3" and a track man: sprinter and jumper) went high above him and really hammered it. Like a volleyball spike. I don't know how Ruwet ever managed to hold onto it. But he did.

(Left, John Timm catches a pass at Fuessenich Park on a different day, against a different team.)

Steve Bogart: "Dick's completed 2 long passes to Ruwet at the end of the game. . . I was the

DB, and they had two guys wide open in the end zone on the last play. . . I went with one guy inside. Timm cut outside and was wide open. Germano completed the pass. And we lost 20-18. . . Argh!"

Though most of the games that the Dick's flag football team won were by lopsided scores, they all weren't. Fierce rivalries built over the years, especially with Regency Lounge and The Place.

Butch Seitz: "I remember catching a winning touchdown pass against Regency Lounge for the championship. Charlie Giampaolo was guarding me. He used to play for us. I caught the pass, but we won because we played together."

John Ocain in *The Torrington Register* on that game and play: "Regency went ahead 30-28 with about a minute to go and seemingly had the game won. Dick's started from the 10 after the score and after losing a yard on the first play, quarterback Chris Germano lofted a pass that Butch Seitz took over his shoulder without breaking stride and outran Charlie Giampaolo for a 59-yard scoring play."

Sidebar from Eddie Janssen: "The officials, John Ocain and Joe Interlandi, used to hate to see us win. One of them warned the other team, 'Watch out for the double reverse.' So we ran a fake one and scored."

Sidebar #2, Speculation: Why the hate for Dick's? Was it only envy? A desire to see the mighty brought low? Perhaps. And perhaps part of it was the idea that there must be something amiss. That no team can win *that* often, legitimately. Which gave rise to the rumor that at least one of Dick's stars was putting something on his flags to make them harder to pull. Tape? Slow drying glue? Today the accusation might be steroid use. Mox nix. . .

Butch Seitz: "I remember John Ocain saying it was a 'pleasure' to ref our games. After the Regency game we went to Dick's, and there was this insurance guy sitting at the bar. Bald guy who drank Bud, I forget his name. He asked us if we just beat LARC. Funny guy."

Eddie Janssen: "Regency and The Place were always wars. They weren't games. . . Right after the game was the worst time. Shaking hands with a team you just beat. I always expected someone to take a shot. But they never did. At the bar later it was OK."

George Perlotto: "My playings years in the Torrington Flag Football League were from 1964 to 1984, the majority of which I played for-and-against Dick's Restaurant. Those years I played for Dick's were the most memorable since following those Monday and Sunday games we all met at Dick's for food, drink, and game talk. It was truly a terrific brotherhood. Dick's was far more than a team sponsor. It was a lifestyle."

Len Lopardo: "I played *against* Dick's in the beginning. George (Perlotto) was the quarterback, and I was a split end. We had close games. Playing *for* Dick's came into play because we both played softball for the Bake Shop. Many of the guys on Dick's played with us including Charles and Eddie Janssen. The many years that followed became the best of our lives. Those 2 local teams (Bake Shop & Dick's) had many men that had grown up together. . . Dick's was a team that played every game. Each person had a role. All of the man had pride and respect for each other. Everyone gave 100%. We became a Band Of Brothers."

(On left, Dick's Tom "Gas" Petrovits, with Torin and the Fuessenich Park bleachers in the background and his "flags" streaming, walks south towards perhaps the huddle, certainly towards his teammates, his Band Of Brothers.)

The Brotherhood. All for one, one for all. Eddie Janssen: "I never saw Charlie Turina mad. Except one time. Another player called John Timm 'a fu*king ni**er,' and Charlie started for him. John stopped Charlie and told him to let it go."

Brotherhood. Teammates sticking together.

On September 1, 1983, Dick's honored 15-year player Charlie Turina with a banquet/roast. Turina was leaving for a new life in California. It was a fitting farewell to a long-time Dick's kingpin. And the last year Dick's would field a flag football team.

Win or lose, at the end of each season Brook and Billy threw the team a banquet. Butch Seitz: "Billy and Brooklyn were the best sponsors you could have. They always put on a dinner for us at the end of the season. They were *very* good to us."

Though not as well known as the men's team, Dick's had a female softball team that existed for 2 years, 1981-'82. Players such as Pam Duprey, Roni and Sandra Tofield, Pat Lovato, Kathy Barber, Jan Mellom, Denise Schibi, Yvette Clark, Faye Richards, Mary Ann Adamski, Kristine Czapor, et al. compiled a 12-18 record while playing in the "C" Division of the Women's Softball League.

Male, female – Dick's was about inclusion and doing the right thing. Being part of the 20th and 21st centuries.

Though sports were important to Brooklyn and Billy, there was also an appreciation for the academic, scholarly side of life. Neither man had gone to college, but they wanted a younger Torrington generation to have that opportunity. A lasting legacy.

Gail Colangelo: "The Dick's Scholarship came about from a gab session. Brook felt that people in Torrington were getting screwed."

The first scholarship committee included Harry Purcell, Domenic Lombardi, Victor Campean, and Vincent Tucker Jr.

On February 3, 1978, it was announced that a $500 scholarship was open to any 1978 THS graduate. It would be known as "The Dick's Restaurant Scholarship," and it was one of the 5 most valuable of the approximate 50 local scholarships. The order of priorities was listed as financial need, scholarship excellence, extracurricular activity, sportsmanship, and community responsibility. Applicants were asked to submit their qualifications in writing to Dick's. The money would be paid directly to the college.

Golf tournaments and clambakes would be the key fundraisers.

At first, and for a few years thereafter, there was only one scholarship winner. An all-or-nothing proposition. But slowly, as time passed, the fund began awarding multiple winners each year. By the time Brooklyn died in 2016, approximately $500,000 had been distributed to more than 100 local high school students. Winners included Anita Visconti, Mary Perrotti, Jeffrey Oelschlegel, James Thibault, Charlene Sorvillo, Scott Beauregard, Rose Marie Scott, Susan Zaharek, Erin Brewer, Emily Mallick, Jacklyn Okenquist, Tiana DeLorge, Maggie Finn, et al. This scholarship, which was originally only an annual award, eventually evolved to a four year stipend, i.e. the scholarship winners came back every year during their college years to receive additional financial assistance.

For 30 years scholarship winners were honored at a Dick's dinner, and photographs were taken by Kevin Sullivan. Winners were presented their award by the current Torrington mayor, e.g. Mike Conway, Delia Donne, and Owen Quinn.

(Left, Mayor Mary Jane Gryniuk bestows a Dick's scholarship on Erica Marine in 1999.)

R.J. Poniatoski has been the longtime chairman of the fund. Scholarship com-mittee members have varied over the years, but have always been a veritable Who's Who of Torrington.

The fund today is still solvent, although it's no longer raising money through golf tournaments and clam bakes. The money is expected to last 2-3 more years.

(Above, the first scholarship award. Front Row, L-R: Brook, winner Mary Jane Alexa, Billy Colangelo. Back Row: Harry Purcell, Vic Campean, Dom Lombardi.)

Pat Colangelo: "Around 1987, Billy predicted bad times ahead. You could feel the fall-off. Brook kept it going as long as he could."

On Black Monday, October 1987, "a stock market crash of unprecedented size lopped 25% off the Dow Jones Industrial Average," according to Wikipedia. In Torrington, housing sales slowed, local industry/manufacturing continued its exodus. Downtown was no longer a vibrant Thursday night or weekend scene. Many of Dick's earliest regulars were retiring and moving to Florida. The times were a-changing, *fast*. And Dick's was no longer an affordable dining option for many.

I remember complaining to Brooklyn around 1999 about the financial difficulty of having 2 sons in private colleges at the same time. He looked at me like maybe I'd just walked in from Timbuktu, and asked simply, "Are *all* your credit cards *maxed out*?" I knew instantly what he meant. Borrowing from *every* source possible. Many in town had to do it. I didn't. I felt guilty for complaining. This was, after all, a man who gave freely of his time and money. Who fed CL&P workers for free during blizzards under the notion that we were all working class, all one big family. A man who, on the Sunday before Christmas, put out an up-for-grabs dinner and supper with the first drink on-the-house. Hundreds came in-and-out during the course of that day.

Family. Dick's family. Extended family. Family to the extent that people parked in the back and walked in past the grill, through the kitchen, and onto the upper dining tier.

Cheryl Richman Dwyer: "It was very funny parking in the back and bringing 'guests' through the kitchen. Guests would always be so surprised!. . . Dick's always felt like home. There were always familiar people; it felt so comfortable."

In July 2008, Raymond "Brooklyn" Colangelo sold Dick's to Marco and Danira Martel, a father and daughter team from Bristol. Just as he had to promise to the Cooke family in 1967, Brook now extracted a promise that the name wouldn't change. And that the menu would be kept essentially the same. The memorabilia on the bar walls would also remain unless the new owners decided to take it down, in which case the Notre Dame helmet, the footballs, the autographed pictures and posters, the framed baseball cards, etc. would revert back to the Colangelos.

It was an attempt to freeze-frame time. To arrest the passage of years and to keep what reporter Edna Z. Wells once called a "decor steeped in a 1940s-era ambience, and having a sense of durability and permanence." Doreen Cellerino: "I remember the decor. . . Silk flowers, wood paneling. . . Never *ever* changing."

But time marches on. And with Brooklyn no longer tending bar and sharing sports stories. With new faces and names all around, the attempt to waylay time was doomed to fail. In short order, Dick's became Tequila's (below)

which in turn became O'Connor's Public House (below). It is O'Connor's today in 2016 and seems to be doing well.

The sports memorabilia, which the Martels had promised to return, if not being displayed in Dick's, was returned to Gail Colangelo, who in turn recently sold it to a sports memorabilia dealer in another part of the state. The sale included a 1967 seat from Yankee Stadium.

Dick's Restaurant was gone.

✤ ✤ ✤ ✤

The Legacy

Of course, when one thinks of the Dick's legacy, the scholarship winners immediately come to mind. Though Dick's Restaurant is gone, the vision of the Colangelo brothers has helped generations of Torrington teens complete their higher education and prepare themselves for a 21st century world. Many of those once-upon-a-time youngsters have indeed bettered their lives, and now gone on to have children of their own. Who, in turn, will. . .

There's a sports facility thriving high on the East Side called, The Vito "Billy" Colangelo Memorial Sports Complex. It's home to 3 baseball fields and the Torrington Warriors.

Ed Corey: "Sports was the passion of the Colangelo brothers, especially baseball. I am most proud that the Torrington Warriors Youth Football partnered with Jim Zeller and built

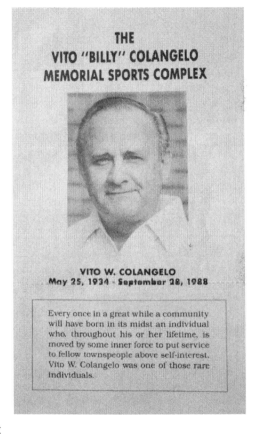

THE VITO "BILLY" COLANGELO MEMORIAL SPORTS COMPLEX

VITO W. COLANGELO
May 25, 1934 - September 28, 1988

Every once in a great while a community will have born in its midst an individual who, throughout his or her lifetime, is moved by some inner force to put service to fellow townspeople above self-interest. Vito W. Colangelo was one of those rare individuals.

their home field at the Vito Colangelo Sports Complex. One of the best families in T-Town."

(Above right, a 1989 informational booklet, printed courtesy of Oddo Print Shop, that lead into the fund raising effort.)

The Colangelo Complex, which was originally targeted with a $250,000 price tag, ultimately has had over $1-million poured into it, all through private fund raising and the tireless work of volunteers such as Jim Zeller Sr. . . The Colangelo name has been a boon.

And, of course, regarding the restaurant's legacy there will always be the memories for those of us who are old enough to have known the people and the place itself. One memory that stands out for me occurred on Saturday, April 3, 2004. We had tickets with another couple to see Arlo Guthrie at the Warner. As it turned out, the UConn men made the National Semifinal in basketball and were scheduled to play Duke that night. Despite knowing it might put me in the doghouse for years, I informed my wife and the other couple that I'd be leaving the concert at intermission and going to Dick's to see the rest of the game, which would already be underway. . . At intermission I was out of my seat so fast the other couple didn't even know I'd left. Got to Dick's and got a seat at the bar. Not a lot of people there, surprisingly. (Below, a different night beneath the tv screen when there *were* a lot of people). . . On the tv court, Emeka

Okafor, Ben Gordon, Josh Boone, & Co. were down, and remained down till there were 24 seconds left in the game. Meanwhile the concert had ended, and the bar filled. Three-deep. Yelling, cheering, back slapping. Key foul shots were sunk, and UConn beat Duke. The bar rocked. A flood of euphoria. People smiling, buying rounds. *Not* heading home anytime soon. . . I've never had a better tv watching experience than that April night at Dick's. It's part of my own take-away, Dick's lasting legacy to me.

Dick's. Was it heaven on earth, or at least on lower East Main? Was everything really *that* perfect? Personal Thoughts: I never heard anyone raise his/her voice in anger, or saw anyone walk out in a huff. Certainly never witnessed a physical fight or 2 people even red-faced and nose-to-nose. Never saw anyone sloppy drunk, or heard complaints about the food, drink, or service. What I *did* witness and hear were smiling faces, laughter, i.e. wall-to-wall bonhomie. A place where you could get away, escape for an hour or two into a friendly, handshaking spot. A place where everyone knew your name, or if they didn't, made you at least feel as if they did. A place called Dick's. And it was here, on lower East Main, once upon a time. . .

Epilogue:
Pat Colangelo: "I miss the people the most. We had good cus-tomers, faithful customers. . . I was in O'Connor's recently and asked to walk through the kitchen. It's exactly the same."

Bingo. And Dick's Restaurant is exactly the same in the memor-ies and thoughts of the thousands of people who experienced it. They dined and drank, and took a part of it home with them forever.

(Above, an original, used bar coaster from Dick's that came home with me)

133

Memories

"Once upon a time there was a tavern,
Where we used to raise a glass or two.
Remember how we laughed away the hours.
And dreamed of all the great things we could do.

Those were the days my friend,
We thought they'd never end.
We'd sing and dance, forever and a day.
We'd live the life we choose,
We'd fight and never lose,
Those were the days, oh yes, those were the days."

          - Mary Hopkin -

(Above, bartender Bruce Kovalaski and Al "Baba" Rinaldi, who owned a barber shop on Franklin Street behind Dick's.)

(Above, Kathy Ahern and John Brennan ham it up at a Dick's clambake at Elks Pond.)

(Above, a clam bake at Elks Pond for fun and to raise scholarship money.)

(Below, a 1980's scene from the banquet hall with some Dick's softball players *and* a much later scene from the main bar with some regulars.)

(Right, Pat Colangelo offers a toast.)

In Memoriam

Matthew "Matty" Considine, 1899-'68
Richard "Dick" Cooke, 1903-'56
Vito "Billy" Colangelo, 1934-'88
Raymond "Brook" Colangelo, 1941-'16

The History Of T.H.S. Swimming
Pt. 1 Warmup – The Earliest Years

(September 24, 2016. I guess I've known for a long time that eventually I'd get around to writing at least a *partial*, history of Torrington High School swimming. I was a competitive swimmer myself for 10 years, earned a varsity at T.H.S. in swimming for all 4 of my undergrad years [captain in 1966], and was the assistant Red Raider swim coach for 5 years during the 1970s. In addition both my sons swam for T.H.S. in the 1990s, i.e. T.H.S. swimming was/is a subject I have a well ingrained knowledge of. I don't know why it's taken me so long to write a "history" of sorts. But, I apologize to any swimmers or coaches I fail to mention here. The subject of T.H.S. swimming was simply too broad, even in this narrow time frame, to get everyone into print. Moreover, regarding the very earliest years, first hand information impossible to come by. . . And now, if everyone is ready, on your marks, get set . . .)

It's never gotten the crowds, press coverage, or glory that the major sports (football, basketball, baseball) have. Cheerleaders have never led megaphone cheers, nor has the band ever sat poolside and given a stirring rendition of the Washington & Lee Swing, i.e. old Red Raider fight song (Below, the 1942 band at Fuessenich for football.)

The Pep Club seldom ran a bus to away meets. *BUT*, for those involved in T.H.S. swimming, none of that was ever expected. Or necessary. The satisfaction came from within. From bettering personal bests. From overcoming lungs that were on fire, arms and legs that ached with lactic acid buildup and felt leadened like a ship's ballast, like anchors threatening to pull a swimmer under. It was always easier to quit: the race, the team. But few ever did. And because they didn't, because dozens have persevered for 60+ years, they've honored themselves *and* given T.H.S. a swimming history.

Although it's difficult to cite exactly when the official start was, i.e. was it when the 64-year continuity *began* (1953)? Or was it when the first THS swim team (1942) took on interscholastic competition in a regular season schedule? *Or*, was it when the first mention occurred of THS students donning swim suits and representing the school (1930)? Regardless, there *was* a start.

Back in the 1990s, Peter Dranginis (T.H.S. 1930) told me that there was a swim team his senior year and that he functioned as captain of what he called that "first ever THS swim team." In 1929-'30 that squad consisted of Art Schmidt, Andy York, Andrew Pavlicovic, Dranginis, et al. and was coached by Bill Hoffman a well known Torrington athlete and coach. According to Captain Dranginis, they practiced 3 nights a week in the Torrington YMCA's old 20-yard pool and had only one duel meet, which was against Gilbert. They lost. In the annual CIAC state meet at Yale (which had started in 1926), Dranginis remembered that they finished 4th, saying that the longer distances in the 25-yard pool killed them. . . I could find no mention of the Gilbert-THS meet in the local press, and I never researched the Yale meet. I took Dranginis at his word; there was no reason not to. He kept a detailed diary and in addition had a phenomenal memory.

During the 1930s, Torrington High School athletes who wanted to swim competitively, swam for the YMCA Seahorses. It wasn't until 1942 that the red-and-white would again churn chlorinated water.

In early winter 1941-'42, Stuart Tobin, a THS senior who'd been swimming for the Y team, went to Principal Richard Hughes' office in the old high school (today Vogel-Wetmore) and asked if he could start a boys swim team at THS. According to Tobin in an 1992 *Register* article, "He (Hughes) practically threw me out. He hated sports." Soon after, Principal Hughes was admitted to the hospital, and Tobin approached Carl Johnson, normally the freshmen supervisor but now Hughes' interim replacement. Johnson told Tobin that he did not have the authority to grant such a request, but suggested he speak to Superintendent John Murphy. Although Murphy himself was new to the position, having replaced the previous superintendent George Vogel only at the start of the 1941-'42 school year, Murphy immediately granted the request. The interview, according to Tobin, only took 5 minutes. Why was the team so easily and quickly approved? Turned out that the superintendent's wife, Doris O'Mara Murphy, had been an Olympic swimmer in the 1924 Games in Paris.

Torrington High swimming in 1942 was vastly different from to-day, rules and stroke technique aside. First, the swimming was done in the Y's old 20-yard pool. (Below, the exterior of the Torrington YMCA of that long ago era.) The pool itself had no starting blocks or

lane lines. The swimmers did not wear facial goggles. Also, there were no uniforms, nor were there even similar bathing suits. Absolutely no warmup suits or sweats. There was, literally, no money. Pearl Harbor had been attacked in December 1941, the country was at war, and the team was on its own to come up with expenses. . . Once the season began, team members had to carpool to away meets (no busses) and chip in for gas. Part of Treasurer Fred Brenker's job was to raise that money. The swimmers also had to rent the YMCA pool for home meets ($10), and if the gate receipts didn't cover the rental, they had to chip in for that too.

Team members included Herb Ginsberg, Jack Kennedy, Louis Basquin, Charley Klambt, Henry O'Connor, Roland LePage, Don Morrison, Charley Zanolli, Peter Basso, Doug Brown, Bill and Tom Burke, Jerome Iffland, John Santo, Joe Ostrosky, Kalahowski, Janiszewski, Newton, and divers Joe Grosso and Tony Asaro.

Stuart Tobin was the Captain, Fred Brenker the President and Treasurer, Jack Kennedy the Vice-President and Secretary, and Joe Videtto the manager. Former swimmer and faculty member Pete Dranginis was the advisor, while well known local swimmers Renny Belli and Frank Janasowski were the coaches. (Below, the 1942 team with Herb Ginsberg in front in jacket and tie, Stuart Tobin alongside him. Fred Brenker in back wearing the white varsity sweater with T.)

There were both Varsity and Jayvee teams, though neither team qualified for a varsity letter since, according to Tobin, there had been a dispute with the Varsity Club. Over what, there's no record of.

It would be great to report that this seminal team finished undefeated. Or at least .500. It didn't. As accurately as I could determine, the team finished 1-7-1, and most of the losses were by lopsided scores. In a meet against Bridgeport, Coach Renny Belli won the 100 Breaststroke, even though he was the coach and had graduated THS seven years earlier (Class Of '35). Regardless, THS lost 45-21.

The Race Times: Because the swim meets were primarily held in 20 yard pools, race distances were multiples of 20. The Jayvee team swam mainly distances of 40 yards. There was even a 20 yard Freestyle against Bristol that Torrington's Doug Brown won in 11.9. Charley Klambt swam the 40 Free in 22.8, Joe Ostrosky won the 60 yard Free in 39.7, and Henry O'Connor churned the 100 Free in 1:06. Winning 100 yard Backstroke times were generally in the 1:20s, though no THS swimmer ever won that event in 1942. . .
Perspective: Though, of course times would get faster over the coming decades, these 1942 clockings were *very* good. Swimming and Torringtonians were a natural blend, i.e. natives did more than just float.

Sidebar: Back in that long ago era, the breaststroke could be swum using *either* an underwater or an over-the-surface recovery, the latter as in today's butterfly stroke. Regardless, it was all called "the breaststroke." The "frog kick" was the only accepted kick. Even though the "dolphin kick" had been invented back in the mid-1930s, it could not be legally combined with an over-the-surface recovery till 1957 (p.163). Bottom Line: Thus when Renny Belli won the 100 yard Breaststroke in 1942 with a time of 1:11.5 (a fine time, indeed), he was probably swimming a conventional type breaststroke, though he *could* have been using a butterfly stroke with a frog kick.

Though that incipient 1942 team was not eminently successful, it must be remembered that they got limited practice time and were essentially on-their-own. Why the season of 1942 did not lead to a nonstop continuation of THS swimming during the next decade, Stuart Tobin didn't know for sure in 1992. But he speculated WWII, with the implication being gas rationing and tight money.

Regardless, Captain Tobin's team brought honor to themselves, THS, and readied the waters for generations of Red Raider swimmers yet to come.

(Right, 4 cheerleaders in 1942 practice on the front lawn of the old Church Street high school. Perhaps they're thinking of the THS swimmers as they practice, but unfortunately it's not likely. . . Below, 3 members of that original 1942 THS swim team pose at the "new" YMCA pool in 1992 on the 50th Anniversary of their seminal season. L-R: Stuart Tobin, Herb Ginsberg, Fred Brenker. In the background the 1992 THS swim team practices.)

The History Of T.H.S. Swimming
Part 2 - The Golden 1950s

(September 30, 2016. It seems as though every T.H.S. sport has had a Golden Era, a time when individual and team records reached unprecedented heights. For Torrington High basketball it was the 1920s, and to a lesser extent the 1940s. The same for football. For cross country it was the 1970s, baseball the 1970s trickling into the early '80s. For swimming, it was the 1950s. Faster swimmers would come along. Records would fall, and fall again many times. *BUT*, the accomplishments of the individuals and teams for that 7 year run would never again be matched, or even seriously approached. . . NOTE: Much thanks to **Bill Ryan**, THS '68, for his 2015 interviews with Joan Rosazza and his overall research of that '56 Olympiad.)

After the 1942 swim season ended, for some inexplicable reason to even those most closely associated with the sport, THS did not assemble another team for a decade. In those intervening years, according to John Murphy's 2013 *Register Citizen* article about the earliest '50's team, high school aged swimmers in that 10 year span continued to swim for the Torrington YMCA. Names like Peter (Bishop) Rosazza, Pete Basso, Phil Kearney, Henry Bianowicz, Johnny Killiany, and Tony Holbrook were all prominent Y natators who would have excelled at THS had there been a team.

But there wasn't.

The change occurred in November 1952. Junior John Murphy (THS 1954) tried out for the THS basketball team and was cut by Coach Connie Donahue. Murphy remembers that Donahue asked him, "Do you belong to the Y?" the implication being that there's a pool there and a swim team (Murphy was already a competitive swimmer), i.e. basketball is *not* your sport. . .

John Murphy's father was superintendent of Torrington schools, and his mother was a former Olympian in swimming. One can very easily imagine the conversation among the Murphys that resulted in the formation of that 1952-'53 THS swim team and the genesis of an uninterrupted run of high school teams. Indeed, Connie Donahue is reputed to have told '54 basketball star Gerry Alaimo that, "It's pretty obvious the only reason Ol' Man Murphy ever started a swim team was because his kid couldn't make the basketball team."

Perhaps an oversimplification. Certainly a tough/humorous assessment. . . *But* the reason aside, fact is, a swim team *was* formed, and Charlie Duggan was appointed coach. Sidebar: No one is sure why Charlie Duggan was appointed. He was the football coach. Had no swimming experience. Many to this day are not even sure he *could* swim. But like the filling of many high school extracurricular positions, Duggan was probably chosen because he wanted the position and no one else did. Simple enough.

On December 5, 1952, *The Torrington Register* ran a preview of the upcoming swim season. Coach Duggan reported that several of the candidates have had good training with the Y team and that "the boys have been concentrating on starts, turns, and general conditioning." Steve Pinney received special recognition as "a veteran Y natator," a swimmer who "should have little difficulty with most of the schoolboy opposition."

Steve Pinney. Though he'd been swimming for the Torrington YMCA, he lived in Goshen and attended Housatonic Valley Regional High School (HVRHS). Superintendent Murphy of the Torrington school system knew Pinney's father, they talked, and the next thing anyone knew, the 6-foot, 175 pound Steve Pinney transferred to THS. A ringer. He became part of what some consider the "first" THS swim team.

(Below, that 1953 THS team. Front Row, L-R: Denis Murphy, Dave Lizotte, Lennie Schmidt, Duke Schneider, Tom Wall, Jack Pollock, Richard "Bullethead" Lake. Back Row: Coach Duggan, Jack Dillon, Captain Dick Juralewicz, Don Craig, John Murphy, Steve Pinney, Donald "Ducky" Nevin, Bill Eichner, Manager Donald Richardson.)

One would expect that a neophyte team would need some breaking in, an adjustment period to the elevated nature of high school vs. YMCA competition. No time was needed. The team finished 8-2, losing only to two Waterbury schools: Crosby and Sacred Heart. They finished 2nd in the state meet behind Sacred Heart and just ahead of Greenwich and Crosby. They finished 4th in the New England meet.

All this first year success was made possible because of several factors. First off, there was Coach Duggan himself. Though by all accounts he started off knowing nothing whatsoever about swimming, he was willing to put in the time. According to *Register* sports columnist Howard Holcomb, "Many nights he (Charley) and his wife (Helen) went over times or over miles of countryside to scout one or another of the teams the Raiders would have to face." Regarding Helen Duggan, some called her "the best swimming assistant coach in the state." John Murphy recounted how in that initial 1953 year, Mrs. Duggan would sit poolside watching the YMCA girls' team train under his mother, the former Olympian Doris Kemple O'Mara Murphy. Helen Duggan would take notes, and the next day the THS boys team would perform the same drills/ workout.

In no small measure were the mermen themselves led by Captain Richard Juralewicz, the only senior on the team. Juralewicz started the year with no competitive swimming experience, and indeed, for most of the season, Coach Duggan rotated the captainship. It wasn't until near the end-of-the-season, after he bettered and proved himself by such feats as swimming the 40 yard Free in 19.9, that Juralewicz was named Captain. . . Another noteworthy "most improved" story

was furnished by freshman Bill Koplar. Koplar as a frosh had been a starting linemen on the Red Raider football team. He, no doubt, started the swim season stiff, sore, and tight. He wound up swimming the 100 Free in 59.8, the 40 Free in 19.8, and surprised everyone in the Sacred Heart meet by stepping onto the diving board and missing first place by two tenths of a point.

Another standout freshman was Tom Wall who bettered his 100 Free time to 57.1 and finished third in the state meet.

Number 1 in '53 was Steve Pinney (on left) who set 2 state high school records and captured the 150 yard Individual Medley at the

New England meet. His 40 yard Free was 18.9, and he landed the 100 yard Breaststroke record in 1:04.2. There's no doubt he was happy about his fortuitous transfer from HVRHS.

NOTE: In the 1950s, the Individual Medley was *not* part of duel meet competition and only appeared in Championship meets. When it was included, it was comprised of only 3 strokes: back, breast, and free, with the backstroke being swum first, i.e. swimmers started *in* the water. Same was true for the Medley Relay, i.e. only 3 strokes. . . The "butterfly" did *not* exist, either as a stroke *or* as an event; the event was called the "100 yard Breaststroke." Clarification: Back then swimmers had the option of using an underwater arm recovery (as in today's breaststroke). *Or*. . . (See p.140 to repeat explanation.)

It was an optimistic Raider squad that began the 1954 season. And why not? They'd lost only senior "Dicky" Juralewicz to graduation and returned experience and talent. (Below, the 1954 team. Note how low the diving board is. It was also *very* stiff, but had to be because of the low ceiling. Diver Erwin Killiany is first on the board. Co-captain Steve Pinney is sitting to the left of the board, Co-captain John Murphy to the right.). . . John Murphy on the fact he was chosen a co-captain: "It's my theory that Charlie Duggan rigged the

vote when he counted the secret ballots for captain – I mean, how could anyone in their right mind vote for me (**I** didn't even vote for me!)? Coach Duggan, I think, was so grateful to my father, the Superintendent of Schools, for hiring him."

John Murphy is selling himself short, and doing it with self-deprecating wit and humor. He was vice president of the senior class, played football for 4 years, and was described in the yearbook as "a good student and one of the boys." He also had command stature, i.e. he was *the* tallest/largest swimmer. It wasn't by accident he wound up at Dartmouth, or was voted co-captain; he earned those honors.

Swimming was part of earning it. Murphy was cited in 1953 as one of the "most improved" by Coach Duggan and had swum the 200 Free in 2:17.5 in '53. A solidly good time.

The THS splashers, led by their co-captains, were poised for another banner year in '54. And by most accounts it was. The team finished 8-2, tied for the state title, and finished 5th in the New England meet. Lake swam a 1:07.8 100 Back; Pinney a 1:03.9 100 Breast, a 1:04.7 100 Back, and a 2:09.4 200 free. Sophomore Wall went 54.2 in the 100 Free, and Murphy a 2:08 (by his own account) in the 200 Free. The team was voted "Luckiest" in the yearbook superlatives. *But* sometimes the ones that got away are remembered most vividly. Overwhelmingly, the swimmers I contacted from that era remembered the 2 losses above all else. John Murphy: "We should have won all our meets senior year. We lost two. The first loss was Sacred Heart."

Tom Wall: "I have never forgotten that we should have broken the Sacred Heart dual meet win streak set over many years. Prior to that big meet in February 1954, we had blackboard strategy meetings as to how we should place our swimmers and finally break the incredible winning streak of SH. We worked many hours on this. I regret greatly that no one foresaw what later became obvious."

The Loss To Sacred Heart: Going into the meet THS had won 6 straight, and Helen Duggan told columnist Hank O'Donnell of the *Waterbury Republican*, "We swim Crosby and Sacred Heart next week, and we're keeping our fingers crossed." Charlie Duggan added that he thought both meets could go down to the final 160 yard Freestyle Relay. . . Coach Duggan also said that the Torrington Y pool had seating for 120 and that 50 seats were already sold to season ticket holders. He felt confident that with a different venue, 200 *more* seats could bed sold. There was *that* much interest.

Turned out the THS-Sacred Heart meet *did* come down to the final relay, though it should *not* have.

Tom Wall: "Just after the diving event, which was the middle of the meet, Jack Pollock, a breaststroker came up to me and said, 'Tom, we can get Steve (Pinney) in the last relay if we keep him out of the 100 yard breaststroke provided Don Everett takes second place. If he does not get the second place, we can use Steve (Right, Co-captain Pinney) in the 100 yard Backstroke to make up the difference.' In other words, we did not need to commit Steve to the 100 yard Breaststroke. As it turned out, Don Everett would have taken a second, and we could have used Steve in the last relay instead of John Murphy (who was slower than Pinney) and easily won the last relay and the meet."

Jack Pollock: "Once Coach Charlie panicked, and insisted on using Steve Pinney in the Breaststroke, the option of keeping Steve available for the relay was gone."

Tom Wall: "As it turned out, Bill Koplar, John Murphy, Don Will, and I lost the last relay to Sacred Heart. And Sacred Heart won the meet 34-33. Sacred Heart Coach Jim Farrar collapsed and had to be resuscitated. There was no joy in Torrington."

No joy indeed. This was a team which was capable of winning and was encouraged to keep their eyes on-the-prize at all times. Jack Pollock: "Coach Duggan's speech every meet was, 'Winning this will make the difference between a good season and a mediocre season.' "

The other loss in 1954 came versus Windham H.S in the waters at Willimantic. What should have been a 1-point victory, became a 3-point loss due to another heartbreaking mental error. Richard "Bullethead" Lake was the fall guy. . . John Murphy: "Richard's head was sort of shaped like a bullet, which was the original reason behind the nickname. We were pretty cruel back then. But stopping with one lap to go – he earned that nickname. . ."

Stopping with one lap to go. In the Windham meet in the 100 yard Backstroke, according to newspaper reports, Richard Lake, "Duggan's backstroke ace," was leading by 5 feet approaching the final turn. "Seeing the diving board overhead caused Lake to think the race was over inasmuch as the races at the Torrington pool end at the diving board," i.e. in 20-yard pools the 100 yard races were 5 laps and in some pools the starting/finishing end varied. According to freestyler Dave Ryan (THS '57), "Bullethead Lake climbed out. Everyone yelled at him. He got back in, but. . ." *The Torrington Register* news coverage stated: "A teammate yelled, 'You've got another lap to go!' and Lake took off in a gallant effort to catch Barber of Windham. The Torrington boy closed the gap considerably, but Barber won by two feet" . . . The winning time was 1:08.3. Lake had swum 1:07.8 in a meet just 2 days before. But "previously" doesn't register points, and what should have been a THS victory in a close meet, turned on another mental error.

Still, 1954 was a successful season. As expected, Steve Pinney won the Service Cup, and all eyes turned towards 1955 and yet another banner year.

Nineteen fifty-five. The year of the Flood. The ravaging of downtown Torrington. But, the only watery inundation that occurred in the *winter* of '55 was the metaphorical tsunami of the THS swim team.

Though superstar Steve Pinney had graduated and moved on to UConn where he would set more records, the THS team had plenty of returning talent, and expectations were realistically high. Richard Lake and David Lizotte were named co-captains. Lake was exclusively a backstroker. Lizotte doubled as a freestyler and diver. Perhaps the most noteworthy change in '55 was the addition of freshman phenom Ray Ostrander. Ostrander entered the THS program having been eminently successful as junior and intermediate swimmer on the Y team. Big things were expected of him. And the 14-year-old Ostrander delivered.

The 1955 team ripped through the opposition that year totally sinking most teams. Windham H.S., which had furnished one of THS's 2 losses in 1954, was beaten easily 43-24. The only serious competition most times came from college freshmen teams, which our local splashers also swam over a several year period: Army, Dartmouth, Trinity, UConn, Union, and even Yale. In addition there were meets with prep school teams such as Hotchkiss.

(Above, the 1955 THS squad. Front Row, L-R: Ray Ostrander, Don
Will, Co-captains Dick Lake and Dave Lizotte, Tom Wall, Bill
Koplar. Middle Row: Erwin Killiany, Bill Eichner, Dennis Murphy,
Don Everett, Roger Bernard, Don Baker. Back Row: Manager Walt
Suski, John Fahey, Gerry Perregaux, Bill Smith, Dave Ryan, Bucky
Lawton, Bob Birney, Billy Mills, Glen Gemelli, Jack Rosazza, Jack
Pollack.)

With victories come the fans, i.e. what Torringtonian doesn't love
a winner? Many followed the team faithfully, and after one swim
meet mention was made in the *Register* that, "Connecticut Route 8
from Torrington to Waterbury has been heavily populated this week
with Torrington High athletic fans."

Betsy Ostrander Quartiero (Ray's sister and a swimmer
herself): "I went to all the meets. It was a family affair. We'd pack up
the car on weekends and go to places like Dartmouth and
Lawrenceville, New Jersey. The whole team was excellent, and it
had an entourage."

In the 1950s, the THS swim team did not travel to away meets by
EJ Kelley bus, but rather by individual cars driven by parents, fans,
and the coach.

Don Baker: "I remember Charlie and Helen Duggan's Pontiac
station wagon well. One year, Duggan, a Union College grad,
arranged for our team to swim against the Union freshmen in Utica.
We whipped them. Returning to Torrington, I'm not sure how many
of us were stuffed into the Pontiac, but I distinctly remember a tire

blowing out and the car veering off the road. Duggan controlled it well and we were all safe. But the experience is seared into my memory cells."

John Murphy: "Parents of the swimmers would get us into their cars and drive us to our away meets. Clement Holbrook, the father of Tony Holbrook, and the head of the Torrington Board of Education, was driving us to one of our swim meets when this song came over the radio: 'She had a dark and roving eye, eye, eye, and her hair hung down in ringalets. . .' The kids in the car knew all the words to the song and we began a singalong, 'She was a nice girl, a proper girl, but one of the rovin' kind' when Mr. Holbrook suddenly turned off the radio. 'Obscene, disgusting,' he said. (Amazing what you remember.) And it was on some of those trips that I actually did learn the words to some 'bawdy' songs. I still remember the words to 'I used to work in Chicago' and 'There once was an Indian maid'. . ."

The other big swimming news in the winter of 1955 was a THS senior, a 17-year-old female sensation named Joan Rosazza who was swimming with the YMCA girl's team. Torrrington, the state of Connecticut, and indeed much of the country had never seen a

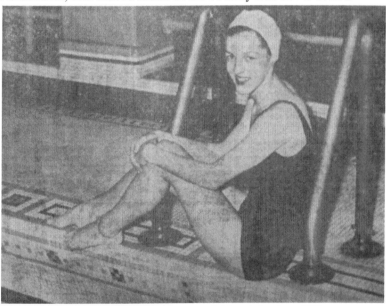

(Above, Joan posing poolside at the local Y)
female freestyler of her caliber. On February 23, 1955, she swam a 59.2 100 yard Freestyle in an exhibition race, breaking her own state

record by almost 2 seconds. The American record at the time was 59.3, and the world's record for women was 58.6, i.e. Joan was only 6-tenths of a second from being the fastest women on the planet, and she was 1-tenth faster than the American record. NOTE: Apparently her 59.2 was not recognized as a new American record because it was done in an exhibition race. . . Tim Dwan (THS '59): "Joan could stay on my tail for the 100 Free, so I knew she could swim Olympic times. I'd swim in exhibition meets alongside her to pace her. No girl could."

Rosazza also held the state record in the 100 butterfly (1:15.3) as well as numerous other state records in distances ranging from 50-to-500 yards. NOTE: Although there was a "butterfly" event for females in YMCA competition, there was none in the boys high school meets. As noted earlier, though schoolboys swam "butterfly" with a frog kick, it was still called "breaststroke."

Though Joan Rosazza was singular in the national and world class times she swam, the Torrington Y team had other female swimmers who, had there been a THS girls' team, would have enjoyed great success. Standout females included Sandra Ruwet and Colleen Murphy along with two 13-year-olds: Beth Eileen Murphy and Marlene DeBrot. All these swimmers were coached by Doris Murphy.

Life for the 1955 THS boys team wasn't all waterproof roses. In early February, according to *The Torrington Register*, Co-captain Dick Lake, Glenn Gemelli, and several others were unable to compete due to being "sidelined for several days with colds and virus infections." Bill Eichner, who occasionally dove, was hurt in a pre-meet practice when he hit the bottom of the pool hard. Sidebar: The "deep" end of the old Y pool was only 6 feet in depth, perhaps 7 or 8 directly under the end of the board. Even though divers could *not* soar to stratospheric heights due to a rigid board and a low ceiling, it *still* wasn't much water to be slicing into.

By mid-February the team was still undefeated at 7-0 and was scheduled to swim a tough 8-1 Crosby team. The week before the 2 schools had squared off in the 300-yard Medley Relay at the Yale Carnival, and the Brass City boys had edged out the Raiders for the win. Positive Note: Torrington had been without Tom Wall who was laid up with the virus.

The THS-Crosby duel meet was held on a Tuesday night, February 16, and what everyone anticipated to be a tough, close match turned out to be exactly that. And more. . . As it played out, several events, which could have gone either way, went the way of "Old Ivy." Torrington freshman Ray Ostrander got beaten in the 100 Free by Crosby star George Galullo (54.6). And the meet was clinched in the next to last event, the 100 Back, when Crosby's Aldo Cipriano and freshman Dave Raymond went one-two, despite the fact that Dick "Bullethead" Lake swam the fastest 100 of his career. Crosby won 35-32.

After the meet Coach Duggan was gracious in his remarks to the press: "Every boy on my team gave me every ounce of energy he had. I have no gripes. We just got beat."

The loss to Crosby forced THS into a tie with Sacred Heart for the Northern conference lead. NOTE: In this era, all Connecticut high school swim teams competed in the State Scholastic Swimming League, which in turn was divided into Northern and Southern Divisions. By March 1955 THS and SHHS were still tied, and a swim off meet was scheduled at Yale's Payne-Whitney pool.

Interest was high, and THS principal John Hogan announced that a bus would be available. Reservations in advance were recommended.

Coach Duggan was also looking ahead. He had his natators travel to New Haven the week before for daily workouts in the Yale pool where they would be swimming against SH. This was seen as a 2-fold advantage over continuing workouts in the old Y pool. First off, the meter board at Yale was springier and almost 2-feet higher than the Torrington Y plank. The divers would have a week to get accustomed to it. Secondly, the 5 added yards each lap was a mental and conditioning factor. Five yards doesn't sound like much, but. . .

Don Baker (on left): "We swam at Yale where Kiphuth, the legendary Yale coach, kept the pool freezing cold to stimulate better performances. Additionally Yale had a practice pool and you had to straddle (naked, I believe) a shower-like device before you could go into the pool. And it was *not* warm either."

Technical Sidebar: In the 1950s teams were only allowed 2 swimmers per event and one relay team. Scoring for the relay was 6 points for 1st, 0 points for 2nd, i.e. it was an all-or-nothing proposition. . . Individual events were scored 5-3-1 with 4th place getting nothing. Under this scoring system if a team won the event they'd get 5 points, but if the other team went 2-3 they get 4 points, i.e. while it was important to have stars and win events, having depth and racking up seconds and thirds was equally as important in the ultimate outcome.

Such a scoring system put a lot of emphasis on strategy, and as the *Register* noted prior to meet time, "Duggan won't say what he's got up his sleeve. . . but you can rest assured both he and Farrar (SH coach) have burned much midnight oil in figuring out this one."

On Tuesday, March 8, with 1000 cheering fans in atten- dance, THS and Sacred Heart met at Yale. The Catholic boys had won 70 straight, duel swimming meets. Their winning streak was on the line. For THS it was a chance to break that streak, avenge last year's heartbreaking loss, and get to state finals against the Southern Division champ, Greenwich H.S.

Once the meet was actually underway, THS jumped out to an ear- ly 6-0 lead by winning the Medley Relay after coming from behind. In the succeeding events the scoring went to 12-3, 13-11, 17-16, etc. i.e. it was always *very* close, with no room for error.

The score was 31-29 going into the last event, the 200 yard Freestyle Relay. Because the winning team would get 6 points and loser none, the meet had come down to this. . . Torrington, which previously had swum a 1:41.3 (25.3 per man), was said "to have the muscle" and was favored. And indeed at the finish they had won easily by 5 yards. . . BUT. . . THEN. . .

Tommy Wall: "Bob Johnson, the announcer, came on and said, 'A very unusual thing has happened. Torrington High School is *disqualified* for not touching (on a turn). . . *BUT.* . . Sacred Heart did *not* touch either.' "

A double disqualification. Unheard of. Unprecedented. Winning streak broken! THS would swim for the state title!

Flashback: In the 1950s and into the 1960s, swimmers even in the freestyle had to touch the wall before turning. This was why many did open turns instead of flip or tumble turns, i.e. without goggles (no one wore goggles till the 1970s) it was difficult to judge the wall, especially at top speed. Good freestylers would sometimes try to coincide their final stroke at the end of each lap with starting the flip, i.e. sort of brush the wall with the hand as the body was already tumbling. Judges would bend over each lane to assure the touch had been made. It was oftentimes difficult to tell, and judgments generally went in favor of the swimmer. But not always. And on this night, *not* for Ray Ostrander of THS. *OR* for Petit of Sacred Heart.

BUT, a win-is-a-win. And this one was sweet. *Very* sweet.

Tim Dwan: "It was bedlam when we beat Sacred Heart."

After the meet, Sacred Heart coach Jim Farrar said: "We had pegged their stars and set up our plan around them. All we had to do was take a second in the 200 yard Freestyle, and we were in. But what happened? Dave Lizotte swam that 200 faster than he ever had had before and took second place. That was the turning point, and we were beaten."

The championship meet against Greenwich H. S. was the sixth meet in ten days, but if the THS mermen were exhausted, they didn't show it. They won 7 out of 8 events in the "shamrock-green waters of Yale's Payne-Whitney pool" according to reporter Don DeCesare, and allowed Greenwich only one first, no seconds, and 6 third places. The final score was 56-11, as dominating a championship win as Connecticut had ever seen. Mention was made by Duggan how hard the boys had worked all year, and added mention was made by reporter DeCesare of the "limited facilities at their disposal in Torrington." Sidebar: This should have been a wakeup call to the Torrington townsfolk to begin planning and building a quality natatorium, a.k.a. a modern swimming pool/ facility, if they wanted to keep up with the times, and to keep winning championships. But, of course, such costly suggestions fell on deaf local ears. . .

In an odd twist of scheduling, by the time the Raider ducks had won the state League championship, they had already won the CIAC State Meet, as well as the New England Meet. Both, like the meet against Greenwich, had been won by wide margins.

It was the trifecta, the triple crown, the grand slam. A first for the young THS team, which had only 3 seasons in-the-books.

Two hundred parents and friends turned out to honor the team at the testimonial at the YMCA sponsored by the Kiwanis Club. The principal speaker was Yale coach Robert Kiphuth. Opening speaker was Sacred Heart coach Jim Farrar who said, "If I had known this (3

THS championships) years ago, you can bet Charlie Duggan wouldn't be here tonight." It was a humorous reference to the fact that Duggan had come to THS from Sacred Heart and that Farrar had been his boss. . . Jackets with a newly designed, embroidered emblem (right) were given to the swimmers, and Register columnist Howard Holcomb mentioned that with the swim team graduating only 2 seniors, "It is entirely possible these folks, and more we hope, will be on hand for a similar affair next season."

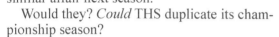

Would they? *Could* THS duplicate its championship season?

The season of 1956 began with high expectations. (Right, some key '56 swimmers. Top Bottom: Bill Koplar, Don Will, Ray Ostrander, Tom Wall) Tommy Wall and Roger Bernard were named co-captains, and the team started its duel meet season on a tear, deep-sixing opponent-after-opponent. And doing it record style. For example, in a meet against Bulkeley of Hartford, THS

swimmers set 1 state record (sophomore Ray Ostrander in the 200

Free, 2:00.4), 3 pool and 3 THS records. Tom Wall swam an 18.7 in the 40 Free breaking Steve Pinney's THS record of 18.9. Swimmers so routinely broke records that pencil, and not ink, was probably used. The team would quickly open up large scoring gaps, and Duggan would wisely get the second stringers into the lineup. Which was good for everyone, i.e. the varsity didn't get overused, while the bench got experience.

Going into the Crosby meet in late January, there was once again great anticipation. Charlie Duggan on January 27: "Duel meet competition is always tougher than that in championship events. You can never tell in advance just what an opposing coach will throw at you. . . A coach must take each event as it comes." Sidebar: Coaches submitted an entry card just before the start of each event. Years later Duggan told me that on at least one occasion (maybe more?) he intentionally scribbled the swimmer's name, making it partly illegible, so that officials could not be sure if it was Wall, Will, or Mills, all of whom are close in spelling. When the official came over for clarification, Duggan told him a name depending on who he now saw swimming for the other team.

THS vs Crosby was always a nailbiter, but not in 1956. THS won 7 out of 8 events (Don Will losing that single event by a tenth of a second), and the final score was 56-13. The 160 yard Medley Relay went a 1:26.4, which was a state record. NOTE: The medley relay in duel meet competition had previously been only 3 strokes, 120 yards (40 yards each swimmer). Now, in 1956 the butterfly leg had been added, though butterfly was still *not* a separate event. . . Sophomore Ray Ostrander swam a sparkling 1:03 in the 100 Backstroke in that meet, and the 160 yard Freestyle Relay (freshman Kevin Gilson, Bill Eichner, Dave Ryan, and Tom Wall) finished in 1:18.5, i.e. 19.6 per man.

No one seriously challenged the Torrington team in '56 with the lone exception of the Yale freshmen who beat them. Ray Ostrander: "Our only real competition was college freshmen teams. They were showcasing us." NOTE: The official final duel meet record of the 1956 team was listed as 14-1, though if the Yale loss is not tallied in and only interscholastic, schoolboy competition included, then the '56 team finished undefeated, 14-0.

In the CIAC State Meet, THS won the state title with 67 points, the most ever by a winning team. Out of the 8 events, Torrington swimmers won 5. Tom Wall won the 100 Free by 4 yards in 53.0, with freshman Kevin Gilson second in 55.8. Ray Ostrander in the 100 Back got tangled in the lane lines, but "put on a burst of speed" and won in 1:02.2. NOTE: In 1956 backstrokers did flip turns, though the flip was different than today's, and backstrokers did not (could not) dolphin their bodies underwater off the turn or start. . . In that same meet, the 200 Freestyle Relay team of Don Will, Bill Eichner, Kevin Gilson, and Bill Koplar won in 1:38.3 (24.6 per man). Sidebar: In 1956 the national high school record was 1:35.3 by New Tier High School of Oak Park, Illinois. And while THS didn't beat that national mark, they could have come much closer with Wall (23.8 in the 50 from a dead start) and Ostrander in the relay lineup.

For the New England Meet at Andover Academy, THS arrived a day early and stayed overnight. Refreshed and ready to swim, they repeated their '55 victory and won another NE Championship. Tom Wall took gold in the 100 Free in the fine time of 52.9. Sidebar: The Connecticut high school record was 52.5 and was set in 1937 by Dave Tyler of Hartford Public.

(Above, a bow-tied Charlie Duggan stands behind 5 THS swimmers who were named High School All Americans for the 1956 season. L-R: Bill Eichner, Bill Koplar, Don Will, Tom Wall, Ray Ostrander.)

   While the THS boys had just swept the triple crown (duel meet champion, CIAC State Meet winners, and New England champs) for the second year in a row, Joan Rosazza was making some waves of her own as a freshman at Purdue University. Flashback: While at THS, she had seen Purdue swimmers at the AAU Nationals in Florida and decided that the Indiana school would be a good place to go. Even though the college offered no athletic scholarships for women, it was the only college Rosazza applied to. NOTE: Though matriculated at Purdue, Rosazza and her teammates swam for the Lafayette Swim Club, as Purdue did *not* have a women's team.
   Nineteen fifty-six was an Olympic year, and the Olympic trials were held at the outdoor Brennan Pool in Detroit, Michigan, starting the second week of August. Swimming at a world caliber level, Joan Rosazza placed second in the 100 meter Freestyle finals in 1:05.2, a tenth of a second behind the winner. NOTE: 100 meters is equal to 109.36 yards, i.e. it's almost 10 yards longer. . . That silver medal finish automatically put her on the women's 4x100 Freestyle Relay Team.
   Joan Rosazza was an Olympian! Torrington's first, and only to this day. (Below, the 1956 United States Olympic Women's Swim Team. Rosazza is in the front row, second from the left)

   Rosazza also tried qualifying for the Olympic Team in the 400 meter Freestyle, but finished 8th in the finals, almost 16 seconds behind the winner, i.e. distance swimming was not her forte.

   The 1956 "summer" Olympics were held in Melbourne, Australia, from November 22 to December 7. Prior to that, Joan trained back in

Indiana, and when she came home, at Yale's Payne-Whitney pool on an invitation from Robert Kiphuth himself.

When the autumn leaves had fallen, and winter's icy glare stared down parts of the United States, Joan and her teammates boarded a plane and flew to Melbourne, Australia, via Hawaii and Fiji. It was the Australian summer and time for the Games of the XVI Olympiad.

In the 100 meter finals, Joan swam in Lane 1, an outside lane and certainly not ideal. In Lane 4 was Australian Dawn Fraser, a swimmer whose times were unrealistically approachable by the rest of the field. BUT, there was always 2nd or 3rd place, both realistically within Rosazza's swimming reach.

(Below, Joan Rosazza swimming in the Melbourne Olympics.)

Who's to say why the breaks fall when-and-where they do. On one hand Rosazza swam magnificently in her wavy, outside lane. On the other hand, she needed one less tenth-of-a-second to medal. A tenth that for some reason was denied her on this day. She finished 4th in 1:05.2, the same time she'd swum in the trials. Third place went to Australia's Faith Leech in 1:05.1. Australian swimmer Lorraine Crapp was 2nd in 1:02.3. And, as expected, Australian Dawn Fraser won. Her time 1:02.0 was a new world and Olympic record.

With Aussies taking the first 3 places in the 100 Free, and those same swimmers part of the Australian 4x100 Free relay team, again, it was pretty much a foregone conclusion who would win relay gold. Sticking to the pre-written script, Dawn Fraser got the Australians a 2.3 second lead, and though the American women came back on the third lap and briefly held the lead, when anchor swimmer Joan Rosazza took off, she was behind by .8 seconds and lost another second on top of that to the faster Lorraine Crapp. Australia got gold in 4:17.1, a new world and Olympic record. The Americans, anchored by Rosazza, finished in 4:19.2, which also bettered the previous world and Olympic record. A truly great race for those top 2 teams.

It was an Olympic medal for Joan and her swimmates. (Joan's silver medal on the previous page.)

Joan Rosazza (rhetorical question, years later): "How did a girl, raised in a town with no sports for girls, get to stand on the medal box at the Olympics and receive a Silver Medal from the Prince of Denmark? Not on her own. . ."

Sidebar: Despite Joan Rosazza's sterling example, it still would be *over* 30 years (the late 1980s) before there would be a *girls'* swim team at THS.

When Joan returned to Torrington in mid-December '56, naturally there was a hero's welcome. It began with a motorcade starting from East Main and Torringford West. There was a police escort, and the caravan included the THS band under drum major Tim Dwan and director David Wheeler. A stand in front of City Hall had been erected by the Park Department, and Renny Belli and Marvin Maskowsky were among the many speakers. Joan was given a ceremonial key to the city by acting mayor Ralph Sabia (below). And

under blue skies and a warm December sun, amidst several hundred well-wishing city residents, Joan Rosazza thanked everyone, singled out her parents for special praise ("They went without things so I could swim, and they always gave me encouragement."), and took her place at the top of Torrington's pantheon of sports legends. A zenith position she has not relinquished to this day.

✣ ✣ ✣ ✣

The next year, 1957 (Right, an original pinback), found the THS tankmen minus key personnel through graduation. Glenn Gemelli was reported to be out for a month because of an auto accident. *But* all was not lost as the squad still had depth and was returning Kevin Gilson, Don Will, and Ray Ostrander, i.e. The Big Three.

In early January 1957, despite the fact that the team had not even gotten wet yet in competition, they were undefeated at 4-0. Explanation: Four teams: Meriden, New London, Portland, and Woodrow Wilson, rather than swim against the THS juggernaut, had graciously stepped aside and forfeited. **Tim Dwan**: "High schools didn't want to swim us. Colleges wanted to schedule us, hoping to attract our All-American swimmers to their schools." **Glenn Gemelli**: "Because of the quality of our team, we wound up swimming against many college freshmen teams like Dartmouth. *That* basically opened the channel for me to go there."

The first meet of the season was against Bristol H.S., and that contest set the tone for the season. THS swept the first 7 events with sophomore Gilson going a 2:08.8 in the 200 Free, and Don Will an 18.7 40 Free and a 1:06.5 100 Back. The aqua flash, Ray Ostrander, broke a 20-year-old state record in the 100 Free finishing in 51.7. NOTE: This time was also, obviously, a new THS record, and it would not be beaten for 20 years.

Next up was Middletown, and despite Don Baker, Dave Ryan, Kevin Gilson, and Gerry Perregaux all being out "for one reason or another," THS won its 21st duel meet in-a-row against schoolboy

161

competition. The last high school to defeat THS was Crosby back in 1955.

On January 25 (Ray Ostrander's birthday), THS met Crosby in what Charlie Duggan predicted would be "a close one." It was anticipated that Glenn Gemelli would still be out, but the day before the meet, Gemelli got a last minute go-ahead from his doctor, got one practice session in, then squared off against the Waterbury team in their pool. . . After the diving, THS was up by a narrow 20-15, when Coach Duggan boldly decided to go for broke. He used his best swimmers in the next few events and in doing so sacrificed the last relay. But, those swimmers came through, and at shower time it was THS 40-29, i.e. 22 Ws in-a-row.

In the next meet, a THS swimmer was disqualified in the breast-stroke for an illegal turn, i.e. a rare occurrence. The reliable Dave Ryan won the 100 Free in 59.4, and the winning streak continued.

In early February fans were told they could attend the swim meet, which began at 7 p.m., and *still* go to the THS basketball at the Armory, which began at 8. NOTE: Swim meets in the 1950s lasted about an hour, i.e. they were much shorter than today, There were fewer events, fewer swimmers (2 per team in each event, instead of today's 3), fewer dives and divers, and finally there were no long distance races. Whether or not basketball fans would *want* to go to a swim meet was another matter. . . The seating area in the old Y pool ran about 10 yards down each side starting at the deep end. The space was narrow and cramped, filled with folding chairs, benches, and shoulder-to-shoulder people. Many would be standing, some in the doorway backed up into the hallway. The ceiling was low, and the space intentionally *hot* (for the swimmers). During swim meets there was almost a visual haze in the room much like a sauna.

Betsy Ostrander Quartiero: "It was hot and fun; we got good crowds. You'd see the same people at every meet. . . The smell of chlorine has never left me. I liked that smell."

Mary Ann Dwan Borla: "There was that stinky chlorine smell, and the sweat of the audience."

In a meet against Windham, Ray Ostrander swam an astounding 1:56.9 in the 200 Free, beating his own state record by nearly 3 seconds. Sidebar: Like his 100 Free time, his 200 Free record would not be beaten as a THS record for 20 years. In that same meet, Don Will churned an 18.5 in the 40 Free and Bill Mills clocked a 1:04.8 in the 100 Back. Superior times. . . Not to be outdone, the 160 yard

Medley Relay of Mills, Erwin Killiany, Baker, and Gilson jetted to a 1:26.2 finish, *another* new state record!

(Below, the state record breakers in the Windham meet. L-R: Ostrander, Baker, Killiany, Gilson, Bill Mills.)

Next up was Hartford Public, which became #26 in-a-row. On route to the victory, Ostrander swam a 1:01.4 100 Back, i.e. there was no stroke he hadn't mastered. Against Manchester Ostrander (get the pencil out), set a new state record in the 40 Free of 17.8, shattering the old mark of 18.3 by Sacred Heart's Walt Shannon in '53. . . *BUT*, the most revolutionary state and THS record by Ostrander came later against Manchester when the indomitable junior swam a 1:01.6 in the 100 Breaststroke. It wasn't just that this time beat former Red Raider Steve Pinney's record of 1:03.9 by over 2 seconds. It was *how* it was done. Pinney had swum "breaststroke" using a butterfly stroke with a frog kick (explained on p.145). Ostrander now used butterfly stroke with a *dolphin kick*, which had been illegal until this 1957 season. NOTE: Though what Ostrander swam was today's "butterfly" and *not* the modern breaststroke, it would *still* be called the "breaststroke" in 1957, though not for much longer.

Two things happened next which had never happened before in the history of THS swimming. And would never happen again. THS swimmers swam in the CIAC State Meet one day. Showered, dressed, packed their suits and towels, left, crossed Connecticut, passed through New York and swam the very next day in the Eastern Interscholastic Swim Meet in Lawrenceville, NJ (south of Princeton). Two championship meets back-to-back. Many miles of travel. No rest. No recovery time. And 2 days after *that*, THS would have a tough meet against perennial rival Sacred Heart.

The THS swimmers were fast, as everyone knew. But were they iron men too?

In the CIAC Meet held at UConn, THS was greeted by many familiar faces. Maurice Hoben, the Torrington Y coach, was the chief timer for the trials. Former THSers, and now UConn students, Tom Burke, John Walsh, Terry Ganem, and Skip Savage were there in force cheering on the Raiders. . . It turned out to be Torrington's day and they won that CIAC Meet by 16 points. The 200 Medley Relay swam a fine 1:52.8. On a down note it was noted that Kevin Gilson's performance, according to the *Register*, "was somewhat below par due to a back injury suffered a week ago when he miscalculated a

dive off the high board and landed on his back. He was treated by the UConn trainer Dick Wargo before the evening finals." Why Gilson was diving off a high, 3-meter board was not mentioned.

The next day at the Easterns in New Jersey, a meet that THS had never entered before due to conflicts with the CIAC Meet, each Torrington duck was off his time by 2-3 seconds. The team wound up tied for 2nd place with LaSalle Academy from Providence, RI. THS's only first was Ostrander in the 200 free (2:02.3). Glenn Gemelli (left) was 5th in the diving.

Two days later the always tough Sacred Heart team was defeated 35-34 for the Northern Division title. The final score was not as close as it would seem. Duggan showed mercy towards his old school and did not swim his best available swimmers in the final relay. If he had, the score would have been 42-27. . . This victory over the Hearts was the 32nd consecutive duel meet win for THS.

The next meet was lost to the Dartmouth frosh, though there seems to be some confusion, looking back, if losses to college teams were counted in the streak. No matter. The most important takeaway was that Glenn Gemelli did 6 excellent dives for 6½s & 7s, and along with Don Baker and Bill Mills impressed Dartmouth officials. Before the trio left campus, they filed application forms with the admissions office. Sidebar: Baker and Gemelli were accepted and in the fall were Big Green, Dartmouth freshmen. They joined former Raiders John Murphy, Dick Baldwin, and Jack Conklin who, in fact, had been in the Dartmouth pool stands in '57 cheering them on. Sidebar: Don Baker was a thinking man's swimmer, and one of his teammates gave him, and not Charlie Duggan, credit for working out the strategies and lineups. . .

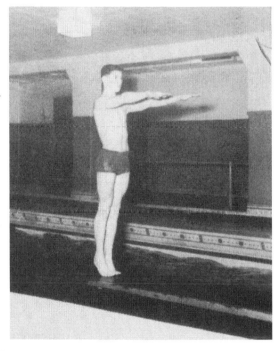

In the New England Meet, THS for the 3rd consecutive year won easily, this time beating LaSalle Academy, which had tied them in the Eastern Meet, by 10 points. The red-and-white 200 Medley Relay of Mills, Killiany, Baker, and Will set a new Connecticut record of 1:51.7. Erwin Killiany was 2nd in the diving.

Erwin Killiany. That rare combination of swimmer *and* diver. (Above, Killiany on the board.) Don Baker: "I remember Irwin Killiany swimming at least four laps of the 20 yard 'Y' pool without coming up for a breath." One of the best swimmers on the team challenged Erwin to an underwater contest, and lost. . . Erwin was part of the medley relay because he could swim a 20.9 40 Fly, which was a superior time. . . On the board, he usually beat Glenn Gemelli, though not always.

Mary Ann Dwan Borla: "Erwin was a very funny guy. He wouldn't care if he beat Gemelli or not. Erwin dove for the love of it. . . Back in those days in the small gym at the Y there was a balcony with a railing. Erwin would jump from the top of the railing onto a trampoline below. He was utterly fearless."

There was no one to coach the 2 divers. As little as Charlie Duggan knew about swimming technique, he knew even less about diving. According to Glenn Gemelli, he himself had been a YMCA Junior Leader and did a lot of gymnastics. On the Y swim team as a youngster he was coached by Art Schmidt. Later, when he and Erwin (Left, Killiany in the middle of a flip in pike. Note that his feet are near the ceiling.) dove for THS, they *might* have helped/ coached each other. Gemelli wasn't sure. He did recall getting some transitory help from a Yale coach during THS's brief training stint there. . . One thing Gemelli did vividly recall was the low ceiling. "When I did a reverse with a half twist, I had my hand on the ceiling (at the apex of the dive). My arm would flex on the ceiling in the twisting part of the dive. I might have pushed off a few times." Gemelli was a pure diver and did not double in swimming as Killiany did. Nor did he dive out of a love for it. Glenn Gemelli: "I was apprehensive after I whacked my head (on the board) a couple of times. After I hit my nose on the board at Hotchkiss, Billy Mills started calling me 'Nose,' which didn't help. I'd get through the nervousness, but I had peaks and valleys in my confidence. I didn't have the passion. My passion was skiing."

With a victory at the New England Meet, THS for the third consecutive year won the triple crown (League, CIAC Meet, New England Meet). It would never happen again.

Columnist Howard Holcomb: "I can truly testify that they (THS swimmers) are true champions. The boys retain enough teenage sparkle to be interesting, but we have found them also to be gentlemen when away from home. They are modest winners, casual losers."

❖ ❖ ❖ ❖

Nineteen fifty-eight. The senior year of Ray Ostrander, simply the greatest THS swimmer of the 1950s. Mary Ann Dwan Borla: "Ray Ostrander, he was something else. If you missed the start, you missed the race," i.e. it was over when Ostrander swam, almost before it began. Certainly in the 40 yard Free.

Ostrander was just plain fast. In all the strokes. In Tim Dwan's words "a lights out swimmer."

The season was off to a seemingly slow start, i.e. the THS basketball team had already won 9 games by the January 10, 1958, swim announcement that the season would open with the Army (West Point) freshmen team.

Army. The very name would have

Torrington High Swimming Team Opens Season Against Army Plebes

The Torrington High School terrington high 24 sports

The Torrington High School swimming team, state and New England champions for the past three seasons, opens its dual meet season tomorrow afternoon. The Red Raiders, coached by Charley Duggan, will oppose the Army Plebes at 1:30 at West Point.

It is the first time a Torrington team has competed at the Point. The boys will leave tomorrow morning at 8:30 and will dine with other athletes at noon in a training meal. After the meet, the Raiders will be guests of the Corps of Cadets at 6:30 supper.

The squad will return tomorrow night following the evening meal.

Coach Duggan has announced the following probable starting lineup. Medley relay — John Hubbard, Tony Holbrook, Jack Rosazza and Kevin Gilson.

200 - yard freestyle — Dick Suski and Co-Capt. Ray Ostrander.

100 - yard conventional breast-stroke—Tony Holbrook and Renny Belli or Alan McKenzie.

50-yard freestyle — Gilson and Ernie Brown.

Diving — McKenzie and Maurice Hoben or Joe Germano.

100 - yard freestyle — Co-Capt. Tony Lockwood and Brown.

100 - yard butterfly — Rosazza and Tim Dwan.

100 - yard backstroke — Ostrander and Hubbard or Bill Smith.

Freestyle relay — Bob Eichner, Jim Bernard, Dwan and Jim Lamoin.

been enough to cause most high school teams to forfeit. Not Torrington. Though the team was not as strong as in the past 3 years, THS was still formidable and always looking for new challenges, new swimming horizons.

The Raiders left town 8:30 Saturday morning, had lunch with the Army swimmers, were given a tour of the West Point buildings by cadet sophomore (3rd classman) Jack Misura who was a former THS athlete. And after the meet the Red-and-White dined with the Corps Of Cadets in Washington Hall at 6:30. The Meet Itself: Despite winning 5 of 9 events, THS fell 40-37, a narrow loss on the Hudson.

New names, previously unseen in finish results, were beginning to appear: Tony Lockwood, Tim Dwan, Bob Eichner, Ernie Brown, et al. Against Bulkeley of Hartford, a key swimming moment occurred when a new event, the 100 yard Butterfly, was swum for the first time in regular, duel meet competition. It was won by Griffin of Bulkeley in 1:19. A slow time, but a difficult, taxing stroke that was here to stay.

Against the UConn frosh, Ostrander won the 100 Back in 1:02, and THS won the meet.

Next up was the always powerful Crosby. The fans turned out, and the Crosby stands were packed. THS was up 38-32 going into the final relay and had won 6 of 8 events. Unfortunately Crosby had superior depth, had taken many seconds-and-thirds, and took the last relay. Old Ivy won 40-38 (Relay now counting 8 points.). The most noteworthy thing about the loss was that it snapped a THS winning streak against high school competition of **36**, spanning several years. Thirty-Six! It undoubtedly remains the longest win streak in THS swimming history to this day.

Disastrous news was received near the very end of January. The tall, muscular Kevin Gilson, aside from Ostrander the only other state/NE caliber swimmer, was declared ineligible "because of scholastic difficulties." He was gone for the rest of the season.

One can only imagine how Coach Duggan felt losing one of his two best swimmers. Duggan had the reputation of being a taskmaster and not cutting slack, a hard-headed disciplinarian. But was he really?

Dave Ryan: "Charlie Duggan had a rule about cigarettes. If you got caught, you were thrown off the team. He caught one of the stars, but didn't throw him off. That showed us a lot."

John Murphy: "Bill 'Cheetah' Koplar got caught by Coach Duggan smoking. But rather than kicking him off the team, he put it up to a vote from the swimmers. Guess how *that* vote turned out."

Charlie Duggan once went to Mohawk Mountain and pulled his star Ray Ostrander, who loved skiing, off the mountain. Ostrander: "Charlie just didn't know how to be nice. He'd tell me if he had my skill, he'd be a killer. (pause) I'd always be nice to my opponents. I'd beat people and feel bad. But I would not ease up if I had the lead. I always wanted to see how well I could do."

Sometimes personalities just clash, and that seemed to be the case with Ostrander and Duggan. Different personality types: Duggan, Type A; Ostrander, Type B. . . Off the record, one other person gave me a blistering appraisal of Duggan. And I know from personal experience Charlie Duggan could be tough, play favorites, and hold grudges. BUT, overall I think he was fair, worked hard himself, and was proud of his team and swimmers.

Ray Ostrander was his #1 star. A swimmer who swam all the strokes and could win any event. . . He was 5'11" and 175 pounds. Narrow hips and shoulders. Iron will. Built to swim, with a fire to win. And willing to do what it took. . . Ostrander: "When we swam Hotchkiss, I forget the year (probably sophomore), Tom Wall Sr. got my father and me alone and told me he wanted me to swim at Payne-Whitney during the summer. And to swim with the Yale swimmers. I did. I was naked the whole summer. Everyone in Payne-Whitney walked around naked (it wasn't coed). We

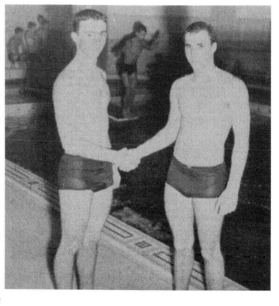

practiced in the 50 meter pool. It really made a difference when I came back." (Above, Co-captains Ostrander and Tony Lockwood.) . .

. Sidebar: Swimming/practicing naked was not unheard of at the time, and I remember doing it on the Torrington YMCA junior team team for one practice. Why, I'm not sure. It *was* fun though. And it felt fast.

With Gilson dry docked, the young Red Raider swimmers had to step up. And they did, somewhat, led by sophomore John Hubbard in his specialty the 100 Back (1:07.5). Against Windham, Ostrander was out with an arm injury (and the breaks keep beating the boys). But Duggan had him in a bathing suit on the sidelines acting as a decoy. It almost worked. Not quite. THS was sunk 39-38.

Against Sacred Heart, Ostrander bounced back, and won the 100 Free in the torrid time of 51.9. Freshman Joe Germano took the diving with Reece Hoben second. THS won. Sidebar: Though the loss of varsity divers Glenn Gemelli and Erwin Killiany via their 1957 graduation hurt the team, Germano and Hoben were excellent young divers and admirably filled the gap.

The duel meet season ended with THS finishing 10-3. Three of the wins were forfeits. Two of the losses were by 1 point. A fine season, but not fine enough to take the League Championship. Nor did the team have the talent level to win the CIAC state meet (won by Crosby), though THS *would have* taken second if one of the swimmers on the 200 yard Freestyle Relay hadn't left the block early (before the incoming swimmer touched). The brightest Raider moment came when Ray Ostrander took gold and broke the state record in the 50 Free (23.2), then doubled down and won the 100 Free in 52.4, which was a CIAC Meet record.

In the New England Meet Ostrander was the sole THS point getter (11 points). He won the 150 yard IM (Individual Medley) in 1:32.4. NOTE 1: The IM still involved only 3 strokes: back, butterfly, free. NOTE 2: Freshman year when Ray was entered in the State IM, he told Charlie Duggan ahead of time that if he won, he wanted 100 pounds of potato chips. He won. Charlie graciously bought him several pounds. . . Ostrander's other event in the New England's was the 100 Free. He was the favorite, the fastest qualifier, and had the lead when he missed his second turn by a wide margin. *The Torrington Register*: "Ostrander stopped, went back, touched, and continued in the race, still managing to cop third place – a disappointing finish for a glorious high school swimming career."

After 3 consecutive years of winning the triple crown (League Champion, CIAC Meet winner, New England winner), THS in 1958 didn't win a single title. The lead line in *The Torrington Register* summed it up succinctly: "The Kings are Dead," and started to elaborate with "The last vestiges of Torrington High School's reign among. . ."

Although the era of unprecedented winning and nationally ranked swimmers was over, the Y pool was *still* filled with water. And there were *more* good teams and Raider ducks *still* to come. . .

Nineteen fifty-nine. Below, the team that would end the decade.

(Front Row, L-R: Bob Gilson, Kevin Gilson, Co-captain Tim Dwan, Dennis Mead, Alan MacKenzie. Second Row: Manager Bill Opper, Pete Grady, Dave Green, Dave Gaylord, John Hubbard, Tom Mettling, Bill Hoffman, Maurice Doolittle, John Eichner, Walt Kozlowski, and Manager Bob White. Third Row: Manager Tom Roman, Terry Dwan, Fred Silano, Ron Peasley, Bob Mills, Charley Vierps, George Ossola, Henry Hoffman, Eddie Cameron, Bob Zande, Raoul Rebillard, Maurice Hoben, Joe German, and Keven Purcell. . . Co-captain Renny Belli Jr. missing.)

The 2 sharks in '59 were Kevin Gilson and freshman Charley Vierps. Though THS beat Bristol in the opening meet, the winning times, other than Gilson (40 Free in 18.5 and 100 Free in 54.1), were nothing noteworthy. They were an indication of a very good, though not championship, season ahead.

Kevin Gilson. It's ironic that the best hands-down swimmer on the team was not the captain, or even a co-or-tri-captain. It was no secret then, or even today among former '50's swimmers, that Kevin Gilson as a teenager was a bit wild. One of his former teammates recently called him "undisciplined" during those years. Gilson

171

himself in a 2015 *Register Citizen* article said of his high school years: "I needed complete structure in my life, or I'd be in trouble." Duggan attempted to provide at least some of that structure and summers had Gilson help him coach clinics at such places as the West Hill Aquatic Camp. . . Physically, Kevin Gilson was 6'4" and muscular. Four year manager Rob White remembers Gilson today "as a powerful swimmer with massive shoulders and back muscles." Certainly he was the *most* statuesque figure on the Torrington, if not the state, swimming scene. . . Bill Dranginis: "I was riding with Gilson in his VW bug. He was driving in the right lane, cut in front of a car in the left lane to make a left turn. The 4 individuals in that car were not happy. They were signaling their displeasure with their

middle fingers and making disparaging remarks about us. They followed us. Kevin pulled over; I thought I was going to die. Kevin got out of the VW, his waist came to about the top of the car. They never slowed down. Kevin Gilson was a very imposing figure."

As the season wore on (Left, Co-captains Tim Dwan and Renny Belli Jr.), Belli set a THS 100 yard Breaststroke record of 1:15, that was shortly beaten by his teammate Alan MacKenzie in 1:14. NOTE: As previously noted, the breaststroke and butterfly were now different strokes and events. Junior John Hubbard turned a 1:05.3 100 Back and sophomore Raoul Rebillard a 1:02.8 100 Fly. The 400 yard Medley Relay team of Hubbard, Belli, Rebillard, and Kevin Gilson at the Yale Carnival (where events were scheduled that were not normally swum by high schoolers) set a state record of 4:19.7. Relay Recap: Gilson trailed by 3 yards when he took off on the anchor leg, caught the Greenwich swimmer on the last turn, and beat him to the finish. It was called "one of Gilson's best performances of his 4 year career." Unfortunately Gilson somehow suffered an arm injury on this day and missed the next 2 meets. . . Flashback: It was around this same time that the Torrington Y used to hold its own Swim Carnival, and I sort-of went head-to-head against Gilson in the 100 Free. Sort-of. I was the fastest 11-12 year old, and was given a head start against Gilson, i.e. I was spotted the difference between my best time and his, probably around 9 seconds. I remember the awful feeling that I would not hold the lead, feeling the power of the water turbulence as we passed going in opposite directions, and how he caught me at the very end and indeed did win. I learned a valuable lesson that day, i.e. it's not easy to hold a lead, especially against Kevin Gilson.

Meanwhile at the University Of Maryland, Ray Ostrander set a national record for collegiate freshman in the 200 yard Individual Medley, 2:15. Don Will at Ohio State turned a 1:10.6 breaststroke leg of the 400 Medley Relay. And Glenn Gemelli broke a pool record in the Dartmouth meet against Amherst. Former THS stars were not flash-in-the-pans, or limited to schoolboy competition. They were now competing on the big stage, in the big pools of the nation and winning.

Back in Torrington, Co-captain Tim Dwan went in too close on a turn, banged his head, and took 8 stitches. The gash was given a spurt of waterproof spray, covered with a bandaid, then a bathing cap was needed to cover it all. The only bathing cap that could be found was at a nearby five-and-dime. The cap, of course, was a girl's and had a large flower on it. Dwan: "Cheez, the ribbing I took."

The 1959 team finished 10-2, placed 3rd in the state meet, and 4th in the New England's.

The swimming decade was over.

❖ ❖ ❖ ❖

Many of the swimmers from this THS swimming era went on to prestigious colleges and professional careers. Ray Ostrander, #1 of the decade, swam for 3 years post-high school at Maryland, but finally had enough. He'd gotten his 100 Free time down to 46+ and his 100 Fly to 51+ (by his own account). But his eye pupils were ruined (later kept him out of aviation/piloting) as a result of 4 hours a day, 7 days a week in heavily chlorinated water. And he didn't enjoy the pressure and resulting nerves, which caused him in a college meet against Pitt to call a time-out, leave the starting block, and throw up into a towel. He was done swimming. He graduated, pursued a teaching career in Connecticut before moving to Stowe, Vermont, where he skied 100 days a year, took skiing groups to Europe, taught at a hockey academy, owned and managed an Italian restaurant, and, in short, enjoyed life out of the water. Ostrander: "I had to learn how to take a shower after I gave up swimming. I was used to just standing under the hot water." His 2 oldest daughters became All American swimmers in college, i.e. Ray himself might have been out-of-the-water, but Ostranders were still winning and bringing home gold.

Tommy Wall: "Don Will went into education and also taught swimming. Bill Mills moved around a lot. He was in education for a short time. He became a policeman and building inspector in the Vail, Colorado area. He later sold heavy equipment throughout the West Coast. Still later, he established a very successful phone business in the ski areas. For the last 20 years or so he has been a farmer on his 35 acre ranch in Paonia, Colorado." . . .Tommy Wall

himself swam with the national champions of Ohio State, and along with John Murphy and Dave Ryan, became a lawyer. Murphy still swims in Masters competition and at 80-years-old is *still* a good distance freestyler. He continues to compete in the THS Alumni Meet (Left Murphy with Tom Wall at the 2013 meet. Photo Credit to Bill Ryan, THS '68) and does flip turns in the 500 Free. . . Dave Ryan took up cycling after law school, did a number of European tours, and won championships. . . Erwin

Killiany stayed in Torrington, married his high school sweetheart Nancy, became a tool and die maker, taught trampoline at one point, was a longtime THS swimming and diving official, and raised a son who himself was an outstanding THS diver. . . Glenn Gemelli made the Air Force a career, and after retirement, flew medium sized charter planes, ferrying fisherman and hunters out to outback spots. He lives on a ranch in Idaho today and loves horses. . . Don Baker studied engineering at Dartmouth and post-college worked for the U.S. Public Health Service as an engineering officer. Later he joined corporate America, worked all over the country, and even today from his home in Virginia does consulting work. . . Tim Dwan briefly returned to THS as an English teacher following a stint as an infantry officer in Vietnam. But it didn't last, eyes-on-the-prize, and he too became a lawyer and eventually a judge. He swam for years in the Empire State Games, won many medals, and today has a daughter and granddaughters who have all achieved much swimming success. . . Kevin Gilson got his degree from Maryland, advanced degrees from West Virginia, then became an associate professor of exercise physiology at UWV as well as being both the men and women's swim team coach for 30 years. A bit of rudderless youth to honored academia. I'm reminded of Shakespeare's Henry IV when the Prince Hal says, "My reformation, glitt'ring o'er my fault,/Shall show more goodly and attract more eyes/Than that which hath no foil to set it off." Reformation. Redemption. Everyone loves a comeback *and* a success story.

Joan Rosazza, after her hero's welcome in Torrington, returned to Purdue, swam for 1 more year, *but* she had, in her own words, "lost the edge." She hung up her swimsuit, and following graduation taught physical education and coached in suburban Chicago. A horrific bicycle accident in Europe in 1960 (she was given last rites) cost her an eye. Bill White: "Joan ended up in a hospital in Rome. My father happened to be on a business trip to Rome while she was in the hospital, so he visited her to show his support and that of all of Torrington." That kind of love and support helped. And Joan, still the winner, *still* the survivor, pulled through. Eventually she moved to Northeast Massachusetts where she continued coaching and teaching. Today she is married to Claire Wilcox, also from Torrington, and together they have 2 adopted daughters. Joan still looks fit and trim. And ready to take on the world.

Postscript

Following the 1959 season and into the post-swimming lives of the swimmers themselves, the THS swim program, meanwhile, went on. There would be many more fine athletes to negotiate the YMCA waters. Many more winning teams, many more records broken. . . It would take awhile. But twenty years later, by the mid-1970s, all those '50's records were shattered. Fifties' legends replaced by newer legends, newer names and faces. . .

Still, those swimming teens from the 1950s had *something.* An inexorable passion, an unshakeable belief that they would win. That somehow despite injuries, sickness, graduations, ineligibility, disqualifications, etc. THS would triumph. And it did. A triumph of talent and will. It was *their* time, *their* championship seasons.

A bright and shining era. And a fluid legacy *not* writ in water.

(Above left, a 1957 championship trophy that sits today in the T.H.S. athletic showcase. The award is one of many swimming honors currently displayed. . . Above right, a young Tom Wall in the 1950s holds yet another championship trophy.)

(Above, the exhibition pool at Yale's Payne Whitney complex as it appeared in February 1954 for the 32nd Annual Yale Swimming Carnival. THS swam in this festival for many years, broke records, and in addition swam in this pool many times during some of the team's most important duel meets. Note the absence of starting blocks, lane lines, and electronic timing devices. But it was state-of-the-art in 1932 when it was built. This pool and the Yale swim team, for 5 decades were under the directorship of Bob Kiphuth. Flashback: I had the honor, along with a couple of other Torrington swimmers, of being yelled at by Mr. Bob Kiphuth around 1960 when we were screwing around. I remember shortly after that, that Torrington swimmers were no longer welcome at Payne Whitney because, as the rumor went, some THS swimmers were fooling and broke a hot water pipe which flooded part of the facility. . . On a much more pleasant and recent note, I spent many Sunday afternoons in this pool facility in the 1990s jogging on the track which runs around the top perimeter. I was working out while my older son was being coached by Connecticut diving guru Jim Pyrch. . . The pool is *still* used today for Yale meets, and for high school championship competition. Many T.H.S. swimmers have won gold, silver, and bronze here in the last 40 years. The THS legacy continuing. . .)

177

Ye Olde Torrington Snapshots
A Photographic Scrapbook

(October 16, 2016. A picture is worth a thousand words. When I think of my life in Torrington, it's images that, to a large part, come to mind. Hundreds/thousands of them. Frozen people, locations, and events that are indelibly imprinted in the neurological synapses of my brain. Many simply because I either took a photo or saw one. What follows comes from my computer iPhoto, and is at least part of my cerebral scrapbook. These are *some* of my favorite, mostly non-family Torrington snapshots. I put them in chronological order for no good reason other than a sense of rightness going from the past to the. . .)

The Migeon Avenue section of Torrington back around the turn of the last century has always appealed to the romantic in me even though it existed long before I was born. I don't think of outhouses, horse manure in the streets, or even a lack of refrigeration, TVs, and other 20th and 21st century conveniences. Rather I think of a slower era, a simpler time full of Victorian richness, beauty, and excesses.

Above is the lower section of Forest Street where it intersects with Migeon. Note that the street is dirt and that the estates of the Bryant family (on the right) and the Migeons (on the left) were still flourishing. Whenever I drive through this area of town, the words of George Eliot in *The Lifted Veil*, at least some of her words, spring to mind: "A new and wondrous scene was breaking upon me: a city under the broad sunshine, that seemed to me as if it were summer sunshine of a long-past century arrested in its course – unrefreshed for ages by dews of night, or the rushing rain-cloud; scorching the dusty, weary, time-eaten grandeur of a people doomed to live on in the stale repetition of memories, like deposed and superannuated kings in their regal gold inwoven tatters." . . . Eliot's prose matching the beauty of the scene. If the reader is willing, please try to imagine, "A long-past century arrested in its course." If *only*, we could go back. . .

At the dawn of the 20th century, times were changing fast. It was the revolution that the Magnificent Ambersons suffered through, i.e. the invention of the automobile and the speeding up of American life. In the below picture taken at Torrington's Main and East Main

intersection, an early parade of cars and motormen, who are walking in long white dusters, is passing streets lined with people. Note the children running out of the way and the horse bolting. Scary, paradigm shifting times. The Allen House is on the left, the Torrington Opera House to the right of that in the far rear. . . Whenever I attend a Torrington Memorial Day Parade in our 21st century, it is the above antique image that at some point pushes in. And I realize that not only have Torringtonians been watching parades in the downtown borough for a *long* time. But also that a bit of the new and unexpected, the *exciting* is to be prized and cherished. It's the right stuff. It heralds the future. . .

While images of Torrington places and scenes are deeply rooted in my memory, ultimately it is the faces of people that dominate. One of the reasons I love the below picture is that I love the faces. Tough

looking bunch. But, *who* are they, *what* are they? I'm not totally sure. I think it's an informal picture of the undefeated 1929 THS football team. Could be 1928. I see Pete Dranginis on the left center, Coach Garey standing in the back far right, and Pivots Pavlicovic second row, far right. BUT, most of the people I leave to the active imagination. The players are wearing different uniforms, have different helmets. I imagine this picture was taken prior to a practice, and now they have the long walk down to Fuessenich Park and back ahead of them. Walking past townspeople of 1920s who would know them and greet them. Perhaps briefly stop them to ask, Do you really think you can beat Naugatuck? Ansonia? The players would have thought they could. And they *did*. Meanwhile, many other teens, such as my 19-year-old father Hudson, were working all over town in factories. These less fortunate youth had to earn wages and help support families (my grandfather had become paralyzed). The above football lads were heroes to them. And when those wearing the red-and-white won, the working teens, and indeed all the townsfolk, were taken out of the grime, oil, and grease of the mills and elevated.

Above, the world famous Hendey Machine Company in 1943 at the height of war production. This factory took up much of the block between Summer and Litchfield Streets, and this entrance was at the intersection of Turner Avenue, Litchfield and New Litchfield Streets (across from TV Lab today). Hendey manufactured lathes and shapers, and was one of the plants that helped Torrington survive the Depression and boom the town during WWII. The mental image I have is not only of this entrance, but of all the workers coming and going like migratory flocks. . . Staying on the factory beat, below, my sister Cynthia and I are sitting at our father's desk in the Needle Shop circa 1953.

I recently found out that this desk survived the closing of the plant and today sits in the appreciative home of Eddie Janssen. It's a comforting thought.

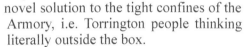

Following WWII, THS basketball had great success, and attracted a correspondingly large following. For those who couldn't attend the games in the late 1940s, our own radio station WTOR started a first-ever broadcast of home matches. Al Vestro, in the top photo, high above the Armory floor calls the play-by-play. I love this photo partly partly because elevating the broadcast platform was such a novel solution to the tight confines of the Armory, i.e. Torrington people thinking literally outside the box.

Left, same late 1940s. Stellar athlete and later well known and popular Torrington downtown businessman Rollie Spino works the THS infield displaying impressive follow through. Photo credit on both photos on this page to Rollie Spino who, in addition to doing well in sports *and* business, was more than just a proficient photographer. He took many informal community pictures when few in the Torrington (or anywhere) did. Those photos are invaluable.

Right, Torrington firemen after battling the Alhambra Theater fire on South Main on December 30, 1949. I note that the chief has a box of Evermore cigars under his arm. Did some grateful citizen give it to him? Is he about to hand them out to his men?. . . In any case, though the theater burned to the ground,  there would be a lot more cinema and live theater yet to come in Torrington. I can't speak for the cigar smoking.

Below, 1953 THS seniors. L-R: Jeanne "Audre" Ratelle, Jean Besozzi, Mary Ann Pavlikovic, and Beverly Christensen with Michaels Jewelers manager Joseph Cusati. The high school girls are looking over a display in St. Peter's Hall put on by Michaels. Part of this photo's appeal to me is that it shows there was a lot more going on in the 1950s with high school students than males playing sports and cheerleaders exhorting them on to victory. It might have been a Father Knows Best era, but not everyone was buying into it. Sidebar: I also love this photo because it portrays Jean Besozzi Rochelt, one of Torrington's longtime *and* better volunteers.

Above, the ravages of the 1955 Flood at the intersection of Franklin and Center Streets. Piles of washed up lumber. Men conferring in the street. Mud, tree roots, etc. On the left is Ficca's Restaurant (today Sawyer's). On the right: Stevens, the Excelsior Laundry, and Italian-American Society. The Flood affected nearly all Torrington residents and was, undoubtedly the worst disaster to ever strike our city. Seven people lost their lives. Most lost power. All who lived through it never forgot it. I still remember standing near the library and watching a river come down Water Street and cross over Main. Relatives who were flooded out moved in with us. It was a time for pulling together. It was our finest hour.

Left: Monday, June 12, 1961. Ground is broken for construction of a new $3.5 million THS. L-R: Superintendent John Hogan, Mayor Anthony Gelormino, Fiore Petricone chairman of the BOE. The school was only approved on a third referendum when plans for a swimming pool were dropped. This school-minus-pool apparently pleased more voting Torringtonians than it upset. . .

Who doesn't remember driver's education with Mr. Frank Faita? Many THS students over the decades got to be better drivers under his careful guidance and endless patience. On right, instructor Faita in the mid-1960s in the front passenger seat with Jimmy Pavlicovic at the wheel, and in the backseat Melanie Dreisbach on left, Alberta Volpe on the right. Jim grew up on Funston Avenue and he was a creative artist and

painter. He probably became a good driver too. . .

From the mid-1960s to the mid-1970s, many Torrington young people served in the military. Right Phil Conforti (THS '66), serving in Panama in June 1967, had "this fellow, " in Phil's words, crawl into his

bunk. Like the cool Torringtonian he is, Phil posed for a picture with him/it before releasing the snake unharmed.

I've had many great Torrington neighbors over the decades, but one of my favorites will always be Egidio "Edgy" Perugini. We lived near each other in the 1970s on Northridge Avenue, though I'd known him since the 1950s. He was a family friend, and he used to repair my "English" bike. Later I bought a tandem, a bicycle-built-for-two, from him. Below, he's on Northridge circa 1978 cruising the North End streets in his 1904 Pope-Waverly, a battery powered car. It was forest green, and Edgy loved that silent auto. He'd give anyone who wanted a ride. He was generous, and a joy giving friend.

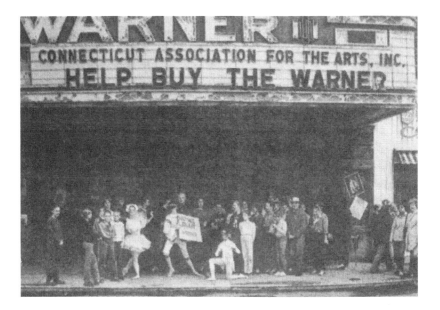

Above, May 1983, a group of Nutmeg Ballet dancers poses in front of the Warner. They're promoting an upcoming performance of Coppelia. Note the marquee. The Warner closed in 1981, and if not for the efforts of a volunteer, non-profit group, the art deco masterpiece, which had fallen into disrepair, would have been razed for a parking lot. The group purchased the building in 1982 with a non-interest loan from businessman Jim Mazzarelli. The cleanup and basic improvements began immediately. Major repairs and upgrades were done piecemeal over the next 2+ decades as money was raised in a variety of ways, including productions like Coppelia. . . Above right, 1992, Harry Arsego and Addo Bonetti start to repair the plaster on the ceiling of the lobby.

Winter 1987. Sliding at West Torrington. Note the absence of a baseball field and any fences. The ski tow rope was long gone by '87, but the steep hill still furnished locals with thrills-and-chills. The Bentleys had a 4-person toboggan, black inner tubes, and 2 Flexible Flyers. Nothing like zipping down this hill from the top, yelling for others to get-out-of-the-way (surprising how many people/kids would mosey up the center of the sloop rather than use the sides), and gliding out to Riverside Avenue. Then repeating. . .

Below, Memorial Day Parade 1989, and a float celebrating the THS centennial, 1889-1989. Man in foreground seems more interested in me and my camera than in the THS float. Torringtonites always were a tough group to impress.

July 1991. Collecting at the Fuessenich gate for the Taste Of Torrington. Paul Grossman on the left in white, Dave Frauenhofer dead center. The event was to benefit the Vito Colangelo Sports Complex, and it got a good turnout. Events included a cruise night, raffle, dancing to Leo Liddle's band, clowns, arts & crafts, et al.

Below, part of the July 1991 setup. There were more tents to the right, as well as vendors in the upper parking lot. It was a wonderful event, and it's a shame that it only was held for a couple of years. Of course, any future holding of such a "Taste" could not be in the new Fuessenich Park as cars and tents would never be allowed on the infield or grass. In a sense, this "Taste" was the predecessor to Main Street Marketplace.

Above, summer 1997. A banner spans Water Street welcoming the Torrington Twisters to town. This was, of course, pre-Torrington Titans, and pre-Nutmeg Ballet on Main. The Nutmeg sign can be seen in the lower right. It was good to see Fuessenich in regular use again. Families and baseball lovers filled the bleachers, and the smell of fried onions, pizza dough, hot dogs, et al. filled the air. The team never won a championship, but college baseball has been here ever since. And now, with beer.

An extremely popular Torrington band, which first formed in the early 1970s, made a comeback in the 1990s. They are still active today, have supported many local causes, and turn out a large crowd whenever they perform. Presenting below: **Apricot Brandy**. L-R: Jimmy "Moon" Maraia, Allen Gunn, Bill Gronsky, Greg Dolecki, drummer Rob Grillo, Jim Buonocore, and keyboardist Joe Bouchard.

St. Patrick's Day 2011, Carbone's Market. Owner and fine Torrington Irishman Tony Renzullo and a leprechaun helper lift one of
his 12-inch corned beef grinders. Quality cold cuts piled high have
made Carbone sandwiches a Torrington cornerstone for many
decades. . . Below, a November 2013 morning. Carbone's fan Roger
Carillo clowns around with his grinder before leaving and enjoying it
at the Yale Bowl, i.e. better a Carbone's grinder at the game than a
hot dog. . .

Above, June 2014, ground breaking ceremony at the soon-to-be renovated Robert Frost Complex at THS. Ed Arum lends some helpful advice to Mario Longobucco, Michelle Cook, and Elinor Carbone on proper shovel technique (compare to p.184). . . Below, THS Athletic Director Mike McKenna in spring 2016 is all smiles. Mike is the latest in a small and proud line of Raider ADs (Connie Donahue, Robert Frost, Charlie McSpiritt, and Newell Porch).

Above, a very sad snapshot in the autumn of 2016 as I write this. The Torrington UConn Branch, which has taught local NW Connecticut students for over 50 years, has closed its doors. I think of the semesters I spent there after the Army, the wonderful faculty, Director Glen Kilner, the idyllic setting, and the fact that a quality education was available just a few miles up the hill and for very little money. What will happen to the facility now, who knows? Hopefully it'll have better luck and success than the UConn men's basketball team has had the last 2 years. And better luck than the University itself has had in utilizing taxpayer money. . .

In Memoriam
July 2014 - October 2016

(October 13, 2016. In my first "Torrington" book I ended with a memorial section paying tribute to the recently departed. Similarly, this tribute will cover those who have died since that first tribute in June 2014. These are the Torrington people I knew: some well, some not so. *Or* ones who had a key impact on our fair city. I didn't/don't know everyone in town, nor am I aware of everyone's contribution. Therefore, it goes without saying, that I'm sure I missed some loving, deserving souls. Apologies in advance for those omissions. We are but dust, imperfect dust at that. But while we're here, and conscious of those who have gone before us, let us look back on those who touched us and moved our city. . .)

Death. The final frontier. It's with a great deal of sadness that I think on some of the following. Yet, some were so filled with life that it's difficult to feel sad, or truly believe they are no longer here.

One of the best known was Marvin "Muff" Maskovsky (1930-'15). He was a man-about-town, an omnipresence that permeated many strata of Torrington life, most notably in recent years the Warner Theatre. My generation remembers Muff best as a popular THS teacher (Left, mid-1960s), and perhaps in the end, that's his best and most lasting tribute. He was a teacher who is positively remembered by many. . . Domenic "Sonny" Toce (1931-'16) was a 1940's THS basketball player, Army vet, UConn graduate, and the reigning patriarch at Toce Tires. He had an extremely fine reputation as a businessman and person. . . Rita Pacheco (1945-'15) after college became a lifelong resident of Torrington. She was well spoken and supremely accomplished, rising to the position of Deputy Commissioner Of Social Services for Connecticut. . . Betty Sanderson (1926-'16) had many talents, not the least of which was her ability to form an original opinion and express it. Over the decades she had literally hundreds of letters-to-the-editor published. Where Betty Sanderson stood on an issue, influenced many. . . Gaida Ribickis (1930-'14) was not a well known name in Torrington. *But*, she was a treasure to those of us who knew her. She was a master seamstress who tackled the toughest projects, and with her alterations, she included humor and bubbling over energy free-of-charge.

Isadore "Izzy" Temkin (1919-'15) was a highly opinionated Torrington character who was my dentist for a decade+. He'd stuff my mouth with cotton, then talk about Torrington and local issues. We frequently disagreed, but it was mostly one-sided as it's tough to talk with a packed mouth. I used to see him in the early morning walking down Route 4 in all sorts of weather on his way to work. He often wore a bowtie, and after he died, it was a large bowtie tribute that his nephew Steven helped orchestrate on a downtown building.

Mahlon Sabo (1943-'14) was our sometimes controversial Chief Of Police. He came to town from New Britain, but adapted well and fast to Torrington. Though we disagreed on occasion, in private conversations I found him personable, thoughtful, well read, and a man with a range of interests outside the TPD. In retirement, he created some very entertaining videos. . . Albina Muschell (1914-'16), Vicky Nietch (1948-'16), Irma Gaioni (1922-'16), and Althea Birden (1926-'16) were all well thought of women whose names were highly regarded. . . I used to see Betty (Mary Elizabeth)

Rivera (1918-'14) at the Historical Society. She listed her occupation as writer and though I never read any of her articles, she was published in a number of prestigious national magazines. She was a local woman who was ahead of her time, and one who set a distinguished example. . .   Jeanne Sands (1940-'16) was not from Torrington, lived most of her life in Harwinton, but wrote for many area newspapers over the years and wrote a plethora of Torrington features. She was a sharp person *and* a fine writer. . . Elmer Kittle (1936-'14) served with the paratroopers of the 187th Airborne Infantry for 8 years during-and-after the Korean War. In Torrington he worked as an operating engineer and was an officer in the United Brothers Club, a proactive Torrington group that helped race relations.

Barry Patterson (1951-'16) was the eponymous owner of an oil company. I remember giving him a hard time back in the 1970s over the price of home heating oil, and Barry telling me that *he* didn't set the price of crude. It was a duh moment, an awakening on my part that changed my thinking forever about gas and oil prices. . . Arthur Oles (1946-16), Gabriele Santoro (1930-15), and Robert Good (1924-'16) were all successful Torrington businessmen whose names became synonymous with their businesses. . . Michael "Mickey" Vinisko (1936-'15), Alfred "Al" Mojon (1931-'15), and Andrew "Andy" Pace (1928-'16) were all well known, well liked Torringtonites. I used to march with Master Sergeant Mojon every Memorial Day and he struck a commanding figure in uniform. Mickey and Andy were regulars at various Torrington sports venues, and everyone seemed to know them. . . Elbert "Al" Becker (1925-'14) was the spunky owner of Al's Shoe Repair on Migeon Avenue. I remember asking him about a decade ago how old he was and being dumbfounded when he said 80. I thought he was late 60s. He was in that kind of great shape: a tribute to hard work, keeping active, and maintaining a good "sole."

Former Torrington Mayor J. Eric Chadwick (1921-'14) was a WWII Navy veteran, an industrialist (Asquared Industries, Inc.), and one of those vital individuals who serve on many boards and do much behind-the-scenes work. He was a striking man with a quiet, best-of-the-best personality. Very likable. Below, L-R, former mayors J. Eric Chadwick, Hodges Waldron, and Mike Conway walk across

Center Bridge in October 1990 as part of Torrington's 250th Anniversary Parade. . . Also on the political beat, Torrington lost Joseph "Joe" Ruwet (1917-'14). Ruwet served on many boards and committees, was elected to the Board Of Public Safety, and served 6-terms as a State Representative for the 64th District. Funny how despite his tremendous accomplishments, 1 have 2 totally unrelated memories of him. The first is how as a swim team parent he faithfully attended all the meets and supported sons Chub and Joel. The second is that of Joe coming to our TAG sale on Northridge Avenue back in 1987 and not buying a child's bicycle (originally purchased at Tommy's). He hovered over it and inspected the black 2-wheeler with training wheels at great length. Then left, later came back, looked it over again. But no sale. Oh well, the Bentleys *still* liked him. And the bike did sell. . . (Below, a 6" campaign giveaway)

RE-ELECT **JOE RUWET** – 64th DISTRICT STATE REP.
"STRENGTH OF EXPERIENCE"

. . . Another politician gone off this transitory earthly campaign trail, is Timothy "Tim" Driscoll (1947-'15). Driscoll had politics in the blood the way most of us have hemoglobin. He served on the City Council, Board Of Ethics, and ran unsuccessfully for mayor and the state senate. But it was on his weekly cable show City Views and his daily interactions at LaMonica's Restaurant that Tim schmoozed and oozed politics and all things Torrington. He was an unmatched "favorite son," at times bigger than life, and lit up the stage at the annual St. Jude's telethon. If ever there was a person who deserved better than he got, especially during the last few years of life, it was Tim. Below, Tim in Burrville in 2007. He was selling hot dogs at the same time he was running for mayor. He sold a damn fine dog.

Torrington people have a way of going all-in for the city. I don't think outsiders ever fully grasp just how much the city can come to

mean to many. Most of the individuals I've already mentioned have had that kind of love and commitment to our city, i.e. they were Torrington spangled with flecks of Litchfield County. Another one who did was Bernard "Bernie" Rubino (1927-'15). Bernie was active in local politics and very active in sports. Near the end of his life he was still selling raffle tickets for P-38 home games at Fuessenich. He was never without a welcoming smile. Above, Bernie collects from former player Frank Bentley. . .

Robert Candiani (1923-'16) was a thorn in the side of local politicians for a long time as head of the Torrington Taxpayer Group. In his latter capacity, Bob was all facts-and-figures; it never got personnel. With his scientific background and logical mind, he made a lot of good, legitimate points and kept the books in public view and under close scrutiny. . . Paul Riccucci (1932-'15) was an accomplished musician who played all over the country, but took time out to play at Torrington's St. Jude's Telethon. . . Edward Zeiner (1923-'15) was a decorated veteran of Patton's 3rd Army and the Battle Of The Bulge. He was the longtime fire marshal in Torrington and was a regular participant in veteran events. . . Maria "Marion"

Vasko (1921-'14) was a former Bradlees employee and a dedicated Torrington volunteer. I encountered her many times at the Senior Center Thrift Shop. She was a hard worker and a sweetheart. . . Anthony "Big Tony" Iovine (1931-'15) ran Big Tony's Newsstand, was a Marine veteran, and was a well known Torrington original. . . Arthur "Art" Perret (1920-'16) was a veteran Army paratrooper and a longtime newspaper columnist. He once told me that he was the one who had named Torrington athletes the "Red Raiders." I saw no reason to doubt him as I had never seen that Raider reference prior to his using it. In his last few decades he was an inveterate letters-to-the-editor writer, and was the master of the terse, pithy zinger. He directed at least one at me. Ouch! Above, is

the start of one of his late 1940's newspaper columns. The byline "Art Perret" guaranteed that the readership would be large. . . Steven

Fox (1979-'15) was not a mover-and-shaker in our borough; he was too young. He was just a good young man, and one I found very likable. He worked as an expert tree trimmer, and did the dangerous work that most of us take for granted. . . From 1950 to the latter part of the 20th century, Anita Marine (1919-'15) ran Quality Hat Store along with her husband James. It was a haberdashery that mixed "quality" with affordability. Even today, my favorite belt came from Quality.

Many people go into making a town, not the least of whom are the personnel in the restaurant/bar/food service business. Elizabeth Woiciechowski (1921-'16) was the wife of Peter Woiciechowski, the legendary founder and a barkeeper of the Berkshire Tavern/Cafe. I don't know how much Mrs. Woiciechowski had to do with the daily Berkshire operations, as it was pretty much a male bastion back in Pete's day. But if she only lent moral support or did the books/ordering that would have been plenty. Restaurants are tough businesses to maintain, and the fact that the "Berk" has last so long speaks highly for all involved. . . Edward Cisowski (1920-'16), along with his brother Anthony, were the founders, owners, and operators of Skee's Diner for almost 40 years. As I write this, the diner is currently undergoing restoration. Below, Skee's Diner as it originally looked 60 years ago on the corner of North Elm and Main. The Cisowski eatery was handsome then, and *will* shine again. . .

Veronica "Von" Rusckowski (1920-'14) I talk about in this book on pp.86-87, just as I talk about Raymond "Brook" Colangelo (1941-'16) in the "Dick's" article. Both Von and Brook once encountered, were never forgotten. . . Andrea "Andy" Dadomo (1925-'16) owned the old Barella's Tavern after Eddie Barella sold out. He renamed it "Andy's." Andy played the accordion at the annual Christmas party, and I think would rather have done that professionally than run a bar. He could be tough and temperamental, but he kept the quality of food and beer high, so we usually let him slide. He could also be a good guy, and when he did talk friendly to us, it was with a slight British accent, words clipped short. Perfect for mimicking when he displeased us, as when he announced he was closing early. . . Michael "Dr. Mike" Maher (1964-'14) was a well known bartender/cook at Dawn's Getaway on lower Winsted Road. He loved life, lived large, and like Andy Dadomo, enjoyed playing music (keyboard). I had him as a student years ago, and. . . Alphonse "Al" Miscikoski (1925-'14) ran Tony's Restaurant for 30+ years with his brother Tony. He had the reputation of working hard, and like the latter two, enjoyed playing music. Below Al on accordion (date and location unknown, but probably post WWII and Water Street). . .

Nicholas "Mike" Samal (1920-'16) was not in food service; he was a tool and die maker. But he *was* a regular at the old Barella's. Like many of his generation he was a WWII vet, but unlike them he'd been captured by the Germans and spent time as a POW. He would sit quietly at the bar and sip his beer. Always a gentleman.

While I've gotten to know many food service people and bartenders well over the years, I've also gotten to know neighbors. And I've had many good ones. Michael "Mike" Merati (1944-'14) was a neighbor at Westledge for a decade or so. Like Tim Driscoll, Mike was a regular at LaMonica's and well entrenched in Torrington politics. . . Laura Sieller (1936-'15) was perhaps the best hearted

neighbor I've ever had. She might have also been the best hearted person I've ever met. She was very active in St. Francis Church, but it just wasn't religion for show. She had a goodness about her that radiated. She would send my wife and me greeting cards to thank us for "this," or congratulate us for "that." Though she fought cancer for years, she would comfort others and was not interested in sympathy or sadness for herself. She almost never failed to stop her car if I was outside to say that our lawn looked good (it seldom did), or to inquire how things were going. In the picture above left, she's just

graciously given a tour to a man who grew up in the house where she now lived. I knew both and arranged it. Though Laura was battling cancer and had good days and bad, she summoned the energy and made everyone feel welcomed. It was a good day. It was a great life. . . Robert Gorski (1953-'15) was a Navy vet, a highly regarded Waterbury Republican employee, and a mechanically inclined tinkerer. . . The most impressive tinkerer and handyman I ever knew was my neighbor for 20 years Andrew "Andy" Angelovich (1939-'15). He was a heavy equipment operator by trade, but that's only where Andy's skills began. He could do anything: build a car from scratch, put on a new roof, install central air conditioning, etc. Below, Andy in the late autumn picking up leaves in a contraption he

built. And yes, it worked, much to my amazement. Andy was a large man with a deep voice and an expansive personality that welcomed everyone. His death was sudden, as was his wife's a month later. Meredith "Pat" Angelovich (1938-'15) was a chemist for the State Of Connecticut. She was bubbly, full of life, and had interests that ranged from painting to gardening to yoga. I don't think she was happy when Andy annexed the space she had planned for an art studio and made it into his professional caliber automobile repair shop. But she made the best of it and simply put her energies into other areas. There were many. They were a great couple, a good fit, wonderful neighbors, and are sorely missed. . . Frank Vitalo (1942-'15) was a neighbor, musician, businessman, and Torrington City Clerk. He knew everyone, and everyone knew him. I remember he used to pay to have his Westledge lawn mowed, then I'd see him at the YMCA working out. This made no sense to me then. *But*, it does now. Frank was smart.

There are people I associate with Torrington High School, some because we were students there at the same time, others because I know what a mark they left. Drew Valla (1948-'16), Paula Bligh Bertrand (1948-'15), Elyse Murelli Paige (1948-'15), Joseph Hickson (1948-'16), and James Juralewicz (1948-'15) were all classmates. It was heart-rending to see their names and faces, *and* so many others, on the "In Memoriam" board at our recent 50th Reunion Sidebar: I  ran into Jimmy Juralewicz in Price Chopper a few years ago. He looked at me, caught my eye, and said, "Don't you say hi to old friends anymore?" Trouble was, I hadn't seen him since high school, and he didn't look remotely like he did back in THS (picture on right). We exchanged pleasantries, but something was missing. I never saw him again. . . Thomas Jerzkiewicz (1945-'15), Louis Cattey (1947-'15), Jim Fichner (1947-16), Robert Ostrander (1946-'15), and James "Jack" Cavaciuti (1947-'15) were upperclassmen at THS when I was a freshman. But they never got older in my mind's eye. . . Peter Yanok (1950-'14), Bryan Carey (1952-'15), and William "Bill" John (1950-'14) were all fine high school athletes and people. Billy John graduated from Rensselaer and became a Senior Vice President of Engineering with a Farmington firm. A very

respected position. He joined my brother and me at the Berkshire (Left, Billy outside the Berk) in 2010 after an Alumni Swim Meet. He might have been a VP, but he was still Billy John the funny teen and now pizza eater to me. . . Edward Fedor (1937-'16) was a Facebook friend, and a longtime acquaintance. I hobnobbed with him for years at Torringford School faculty parties. He was a Navy vet, a head honcho in computers from early on, and an all around good guy. . . Left, Sandy Schenk LaRocco (1949-'14). She was a medical secretary at Opticare. I'd see her occasionally at the supermarket, but it's when we were all together as newlyweds in the early 1970s that I remember her best. Fondue anyone?

A few recently passed athletes graduated before I arrived at THS, but I remember them as if it were yesterday. Tom Andrighetti (1944-'16) was a star football player and later a successful businessman. . . John Eichner (1943-'16) was a fast swimmer and a good looking guy. I watched him compete many times in the old Y pool. He led a varied career that included teaching and being Director Of X-Ray Technology at Middlesex Hospital. He was probably best known in Torrington as the owner of Eichner Real Estate. We talked a couple of years ago at the Warner, and I was saddened to learn he hadn't been well. It's always disheartening to learn that people you looked up to when you're young are not immortal, though John remains large in my memory. . . Gerald "Jerry" Belli (1944-'16), like Eichner, was a swimmer (Left, Jerry in 1962) and a champion in his youth. He worked many years for

SNET, and evenings I'd sometimes catch him and his wife Gaye at Tony's or the Elks. Always with that trademark Belli smile and illuminating personality. Jerry amazed me one Christmas season by playing the piano and leading a women's club in carols. I didn't know he played. He told me he taught himself. Then, I'm sure he smiled.

Though the teens I knew from THS are now senior citizens themselves, a number had parents who lived to ripe old ages and only passed recently. Arthur Cisco (1923-'15) co-owned Cisco Brothers Plumbing and had 3 daughters (Barbara, Linda, Nancy) who I knew. His plumbing business was well regarded in Torrington. . . Paul Hawley (1924-'15), whose son Buddy I worked with at Camp Workcoeman, held many important positions, though it's for his volunteer work with the Boy Scouts that I remember him best. . . Rena Spadaccini (1927-'15) worked at the S&H Green Stamp Store (picture on p.82) and was the mother of my good friend, Dave. . . Gilda Bickford Vedovelli (1927-'14) in the 1960s became only the second female real estate agent in Litchfield County. She opened her own agency and championed the position of women in business. Her older son John (Bickford), a former high ranking IRS official, obviously inherited his business acumen from her. . . Anne Pond Buckley (1924-'15), mother to Biff and Chris, was an originator of the Charlotte Hungerford Hospital art gallery and a volunteer at the CHH gift shop. She was a lovely woman. . . Catherine "Kitty" Paguisco (1922-'16), mother to Barbara and Sherry, also volunteered at the CHH gift shop, was a founding member of the Torringford Volunteer Fire Department Auxiliary, and volunteered at the Lourdes Shrine. She worked for years at Howard's, and along with her husband "Pugie" was a lot of fun. . . Margaret Rendino (1919-'16) mother to Lenny; Gerda Franculli Behlen (1923-'16) mother to Frank, John, and Kathy; and Charles Hartley Connell (1915-'16) father to Hartley (Bud), Candyce, and Sheila – all enjoyed great longevity, and loved and were loved in return.

Finally, there are those who died who were in the educational field, i.e. the ones who left a legacy in the thousands. Though Carmen Troccolo (1920-'14) and Stanley Zega (1923-'16) were not teachers (both worked in maintenance), both men were *very* well known to the student population and extremely well liked and respected. . . Laura Bramen Corcoran (1946-'16) was a teacher for a few years at Torringford School before she and husband Tim moved out of town, and eventually out of state. Many in town still remember her well. . . . Kathleen Healey Gilson (1945-'15) was Torrington born and raised. She taught at HarBur Middle School in Burlington for over 30 years and lived just over the Torrington line in Litchfield. I worked with her for a number of years, and after she retired I asked her how she was enjoying it. She said she wasn't. Such was her dedication and total immersion in the job. . . John Metro (1923-16), Helen Woodford (1927-'15), and William "Bill" Meyer (1922-'15) were all active teachers back in the swinging sixties. Both Meyer and Metro were WWII vets, though it was Helen Woodford who had the intimidation factor going strong, at least with the female students. All 3 were accomplished people and led active lives in retirement. Bill Meyer was still attending Warner productions not long before he died at 92. . . Ena Malahan (1914-'16) lived to be 102 and in her earlier years taught at Torringford School. She was said to be a beautiful woman who dressed to the nines and was loved by everyone. The type of teacher little boys fall in love with.

Mike Bakunis (1942-'16) taught at Oliver Wolcott Tech for 28 years with great success. He had a number of yearbooks dedicated to him and was voted Teacher Of The Year by his peers. After OWTS he taught Adult Education and established an ESL class at Thomaston HS. He'd been a football co-captain at THS and used this to good advantage in adulthood. He coached the midget team and along with Mike Conway broadcast local football and basketball games on Cable 5. I was surprised to learn that he also loved opera and that he and his wife Mitzi were founding members of the Warner Theatre Opera Guild. When I asked him about it, he just shrugged it  off and smiled as if to say, I'm *not* a dumb jock. He also downplayed his battle with cancer and looked thin, but strong, when I talked to him on one of his walks. Above, Mike Bakunis in 1980 making a point in his history/civics/economics class. He had the reputation of sprinkling personal anecdotes and interesting tidbits into his lectures. The kind of teacher every student should have at least once in life. Thousands did, and are inimitably better off because of it.

Terri Cetra Reichen (1950-'16) taught for more than 30 years at East School in Torrington. After she retired, like many teachers not quite ready to kick back, she returned as a substitute. . . I knew Terri for years. She always had an optimistic personality, and she maintained her courage and upbeat aura even after her cancer diagnosis. We were Facebook friends, and Terri really enjoyed interacting with people. She loved talking about riding in her convertible and posting pictures of visiting her daughters, especially Jenna who lives in Washington. She gave me a great recipe for eggplant parmesan, and we chatted about the Culinary Institute, vacations, and other topics. The conversations were always short and light. Then she messaged me one day on Facebook to ask if I was aware of her medical condition. It was something I hadn't wanted to talk about, not being sure what to say. I knew the prognosis wasn't good. But Terri was willing, and actually eager, I think, to get it out in the open between us. She was no coward, but rather met life head on. She told me about her treatments at Dana Farber and was greatly encouraged by her progress. She seemed more worried about husband Fred than herself. . . In one of her last messages, Terri said, "So far, so good." She said that these days she was just happy to play in her gardens. . . One of the last times I saw Terri in person was at a Coe Park

summer concert (above) a couple of years before she died. As always, she was smiling, laughing, full of life. That's how I'll remember her. And how she would want to be remembered. . .

Frank Cimino (1923 -'16) was a teacher, assistant principal, principal, and an all around ball-of-fun. Because he lived next door to my wife's family on Newfield Road, I got to know him on a personal level from the mid-1960s on. He'd join the male family members on Sunday afternoons to play horseshoes. And he was good. He was also one-of-the-guys, and despite being a devote and active church goer, loved a good joke, clean *or* raunchy. He loved to laugh, and he loved to cause others to laugh. . . After my mother-in-law, Helen, became a widow, Frank would bring her his homemade soup and make sure all was well with her. He had a sincere and natural empathy. . . I saw him often at the Y, even after he depended on a cane to get around. He simply would not let physical ailments get him down. . . It was always good to see Frank and to talk to him. He lived large, and has left a larger void with his passing. He is missed.

(Above, Frank Cimino in May 1999 on Torrington's Main Street for Connecticut Bike Weekend. The street was filled with Harleys and other large motorcycles. Along came Frank, at nearly 76-years-old, wearing a vintage helmet and riding his small Honda, which was spewing blue exhaust fumes. It was a perfect Frank Cimino moment.)

(Above, in front of Riverside School in 2008 for an 8th grade reunion of the Class Of 1963. It's a major tribute to Frank Cimino that his former students *still* wanted to get together with him 45 years later. L-R, Front Row: Jeanne Urezzio Liptak, Karen Santore Maturo, Mr. Frank Cimino, Joyce Kost. . . Middle Row: Cynthia Lent VanLoan, Linda Ferris, Thomas Rezendes, Judy Cisco Seldner, Robert Britton, Linda Perlotto. . . Back Row: John Hriczo, Anthony Giglio, Wayne Bovi, Rosanne Alicata. . . NOTE: Paul Arezzini was also at the reunion, but didn't get from the party at the Sunnyside to the school in time for the picture. . . Photo credit to Robert Britain with a special thanks to him for identifying everyone.)

Right, Frank Cimino on the grounds of the Torrington Historical Society in August 2010. It was the annual summer party, and Frank was really enjoying himself. My wife, his longtime neighbor, had just said something to him. I don't recall what it was, but it never took much to get Frank smiling and laughing. Good times came easily to him. And this is my lasting image and memory of him. . .

Epilogue

Once again, the end of a "Torrington" book has been reached. As always, it was a lot of fun for me researching these articles and putting the information into readable form. I know that most of the people I interviewed have grown impatient waiting for the finished product. And I apologize, but that's a major difference between newspaper writing and book writing, i.e. quick vs. slow/delayed gratification. Consolation: Had the major articles here been published in a newspaper, two things are certain. First off, the articles would have been much shorter with many fewer pictures. There is no newspaper I know of that would have granted me the space/column inches these features took. The old *Voice* might have, but that weekly is long gone. . . Secondly, had I been a full-time reporter, no newspaper would have granted me the time some of these articles took to research and write. The topics just aren't important or relevant enough in even the local newspaper game, though they are to me.

I hope readers took note of the date on article about "The Old Fudge House," pp. 68-77. Sorry (big smile), but I couldn't resist. . .

Will there be yet another, a *fifth* "Torrington" book? Yes, unless unforeseen calamity strikes. I had intended to end the series with *Ye Olde*, but there was one article close to my heart that I wanted to write but didn't. I was going to follow the article on T.H.S. Swimming In The 1950s with a feature on T.H.S. Swimming In The **1960s**. But as the 50's piece ran for 33 pages (longest I've ever written), and I knew there was only so much that people wanted to read about swimming, I've had to postpone the 60's piece for another day, another year, another book. It's unfinished business that'll probably see print in 2017. Probably. . .

Till we meet again, live well, live long, prosper, and may the Torrington force be with you.

See you all around. . .

Best this Torrington day!

Paul Bentley

Autumn 2016

Made in the USA
Charleston, SC
15 December 2016